TAX
FREE

by Mark Skousen

Simon and Schuster

New York

This book is sold with the understanding that neither the Author nor the Publisher is engaged in rendering legal or accounting services. Tax information and advice is always subject to new interpretation, court decisions, government rulings and legislation. Questions relevant to the practice of law or accounting should be addressed to a member of those professions. The Author and Publisher specifically disclaim any liability, loss or risk, personal or otherwise, which is incurred as a consequence, directly or indirectly, of the use and application of any of the contents of this work.

SIMON AND SCHUSTER and colophon are trademarks of Simon & Schuster
Manufactured in the United States of America

1 2 3 4 5 6 7 8 9 10

Library of Congress Cataloging in Publication Data

Skousen, Mark.
  Tax free.
  Includes bibliographies and index.
  1. Taxation, Exemption from—Law and legislation—
United States.   I. Title.
KF6375.S55   1982b   343.7305′23   82-16780
                         347.303523

ISBN 0-671-46061-7

Acknowledgments

Oppressive taxation has been the most serious financial problem facing Americans in the postwar period. While inflation may diminish the purchasing power of one's income by as much as 15%, government levies take, on average, 35% of one's income every year. Even with marginal tax cuts, the burden is heavy to bear. My research has been fruitful, however, in discovering ways to reduce, and sometimes even eliminate, this burden.

So it is fitting that my first acknowledgment goes to the Congress of the United States. If I were to give our legislators a backhanded compliment, it would be that without them, this book would be mighty slim!

On a personal note, I would first like to thank my wife and companion in this tedious, time-consuming, and taxing business of writing and publishing books. I had to promise her money, vacations, gifts, and the pledge "This will be my last book" before she finally agreed to the task. Jo Ann spent most of her waking hours editing, rewriting, questioning, and pontificating on the subject of taxation, a wholly disagreeable topic compared to her first loves of children, piano, and literature.

Thanks also to Michael Savage, a very talented tax attorney and friend, for writing the introduction and reviewing the manuscript for any glaring errors. Mr. Savage is the author of the best-seller *Everything You Always Wanted to Know About Taxes,* and is editor of *Taxes Interpreted.* Also, appreciation goes to Adrian Day, Ed Gunther, and Doug Casey, for providing information on living and investing abroad. Finally, I would like to thank Vernon K. Jacobs, editor of *Tax Angles,* for planting the seed for many of the tax ideas contained in this book.

—Mark Skousen

To my brother,
Joel

Contents

8   Contents

━Preface: A New Tax Strategy

by Michael D. Savage

IT IS no secret that the great majority of Americans have little or no understanding of the federal income tax laws and how they work. People who specialize in taxes blame this on Congress for writing such complex laws in the first place. We also blame the Treasury Department, whose long and convoluted regulations hardly provide the "interpretation" that Treasury is obligated to give us. The biggest culprit, of course, is the Internal Revenue Service. Most tax specialists would agree that the IRS never publishes a meaningful explanation of the tax laws, one that actually helps you save taxes.

All these institutions—the Congressional staff, the Treasury, and the IRS—are made up of tax specialists and tax lawyers. Consequently, the tax law is very difficult to grasp, and can only be understood by other tax specialists.

Mark Skousen's book is a refreshing departure from this tradition. Mark does not claim to be a tax specialist. He has just worked hard and learned a lot about taxes. You won't find a word of legalese or tax-lawyer gobbledygook in any of the pages that follow this introduction. But you will learn something about taxes, and how to avoid them.

Tax specialists have another shortcoming, besides their complex writing style. They only know about taxes, and very little about investments! Yet, taxes are paid with *money,* money that you earn or invest. The whole reason for learning more about taxes is to learn how to manage your money so that you will pay less to the government, so that you will have more money left over to achieve your personal goals.

Taxes and money management are inseparable. A tax specialist may tell you, "If you want to cut your tax bill, invest in municipal bonds." That's fine. But what is a municipal bond, where do I find one, which one do I want, and what do I do after I get it? Many tax specialists will respond, "I'm a tax adviser, not an investment adviser." Mark's reputation as an investment adviser requires no embellishment, and in this book he doesn't leave you hanging. If he tells you to invest in municipal bonds, he will go on to tell you how, who, where, and how much. This is not the stuff that tax treatises are made of.

Most tax specialists have another shortcoming. Once they start to write about taxes, they tend to cover the whole field. The Internal Revenue Code is about 2,500 pages long, and sometimes one gets the impression that tax writers would like to top that. Mark has taken a different tack: He has decided to concentrate on one area of the tax law, that of *tax-free income*. The result is a thorough treatment of his subject that is simple to understand and easy to act upon. It is thoroughly informative and useful from page one.

Since taxes began their steady climb two decades ago, taxpayers and tax specialists have looked primarily for *deductions*. We have bought houses to reduce taxes. We have given away our money to eliminate taxes. We have accepted rising real estate assessments and sky-high medical insurance premiums because, after all, they're deductible. We have even paid for tax advice because that, too, is deductible. We have invested in questionable real estate deals, drilled for oil in sand formations, bought railroad cars, donated Bibles and gemstones, and put up money to invent a perpetual motion machine—all because they were tax deductible.

What has been the result? Interest rates on home mortgages are now too high to refinance. We have lost a lot of money in river barges and movie films. And when investments have paid off, we have ended up with *more* taxable income, making it necessary to look for new shelters to offset the income from our old shelters!

Taxpayers, investors, and even some tax specialists are starting to say, *Enough is enough!* Keeping one step ahead of high taxation is not the solution. The solution is to avoid taxes altogether, whether it be taxes on income, estates, corporations, interest, dividends, sales, or personal property. I'm not talking about illegal schemes used to evade taxes, I'm talking about *legitimate exemptions* written into the Tax Code. By following the proper procedures, you *can* earn tax-free income, or income that is tax-deferred for as long as you choose, or income that is taxed at acceptably low rates.

Mark Skousen's book is very timely, perhaps even slightly ahead of its time. Tax-exempt investments, offshore tax strategies, pension plans, and income-splitting devices are some of the approaches that Mark recommends. Indeed, they are the kinds of techniques that are being developed right now in the offices of many tax specialists!

The tax-free strategy is a relatively new weapon in the battle against excessive taxation. We are still feeling our way, wondering what are the best techniques, what is legal, and what is wise. Initially, the result may not be as dramatic as a "4-to-1" shelter. It takes time to become tax-free. But living and investing tax-free, however long it takes, is emerging as the best solution for avoiding high taxes. It is destined to be *the* tax-avoidance approach of the 1980s.

A tax-free movement is in progress. Mark Skousen's book can place you at the forefront.

—Michael D. Savage
Attorney at Law
Washington, D.C.

1

—What This Book Will Do for You

A COLLEAGUE of mine, tax expert Larry Abraham, once told me, "There is not now, nor has there ever been, nor will there ever be, a tax law without legal loopholes." That, in a nutshell, is the basis for *Tax Free: All the Legal Ways to Be Exempt from Federal State and Social Security Taxes.* The need for umbrella protection from growing government levies has never been greater. Fortunately, there are still certain tools available for investors and businesses to use to avoid taxation—and the higher your tax bracket, the greater the possibility is that you can take advantage of the ideas contained in this special report.

WHY THIS BOOK IS UNIQUE

There are, of course, numerous books on the market today on the subject of *tax planning.* Many books have been written on the subject of *tax shelters,* sound investment opportunities that simultaneously offer high write-offs, such as limited partnerships in energy, real estate, research and development, and mining. Other best-sellers have stressed all the legal *deductions* you can claim on your tax return, so that you will not overlook such deductions as automobile and medical expenses, business travel and entertainment, and expenses for an office in the home. Needless to say, tax shelters and personal deductions are very important in overall tax planning.

But until now, no one has written a book exclusively on the subject of *tax-exempt* areas: investments and financial organizations that are simply not subject to current or future taxes. In my research, I was very surprised to learn how many "loopholes" have been created by Congress over the years to provide tax relief for certain special interests. Fortunately, the categories have become so broad that anyone with sufficient funds and know-how can take advantage of them. Tax exemption, once an area only for the rich, is now available to almost all businesses and individual investors. This book will show you the way.

TYPES OF EXEMPTIONS

The history of taxation is replete with examples of exemptions. Take income taxes, for example. Since the beginning of federal income taxes in 1913, an exception has always been made for interest derived from state and local municipal bonds, based on the Constitutional principle of "reciprocal immunity." That is, the federal government cannot tax the bonds of states, and the states in turn cannot tax U.S. Treasury bonds. (The investment opportunities in municipal bonds will be treated in detail in this book.)

Of course, municipal bonds are not the only example of tax-free investing. There are literally hundreds of ways to be exempt from current income taxation. Some of these include deferred annuities and other insurance policies, pension plans, return-of-capital utility dividends, tax-free exchanges in real estate, and, lately, All-Savers Certificates.

But it isn't just *investing* that can be tax-exempt. Many forms of *income* can be exempt from federal taxation. These include certain fringe benefits at work, the personal exemptions (now at $1,000 per person, and bound to rise in the future with inflation), and amazing exclusions for Americans living abroad.

Certain states of the union qualify as tax-exempt areas as well. There are half a dozen states that impose no state income tax, while others require no sales taxes.

A major breakthrough in this book is a whole chapter devoted to the tremendous financial advantages of *tax-exempt organizations*. Very little has been written outlining exactly how these religious, educational, and charitable institutions take advantage of their exemptions from federal, state, and social security taxes.

Over the past year, I have done a great deal of original research, synthesizing myriad documents and data on the subject of tax-exempt investments and businesses. My book, *Tax-Free*, gives you all the basics you need to get started on the road to independence from government assessments.

WHY CONSIDER EXEMPTIONS?

It's not possible, unfortunately, for all your assets to be under the exemption umbrella, so you must still entertain other tax-reduction techniques, such as investment shelters and personal deductions. But tax-exempt investments and businesses should become an increasingly important element of your financial planning.

Here are several major reasons for using tax-exempt areas:

1. *To maintain financial privacy and a low profile.* You reduce your audit potential with the government tax authorities (misnamed the Internal Revenue "Service") because, in many cases, your tax-exempt investments do not have to be reported at all, and in cases where reporting is required, the reporting is often not given a high priority by Treasury agents. Tax-exempt foundations, for instance, handle billions of dollars every year, but are seldom audited by the IRS. Contrast this nonreporting feature with high-profile *deductions* that you may claim on your tax return. Government computers that process returns are set to discover "excessive" deductions, or certain kinds of deductions, and kick out those returns, thereby increasing your chances of an in-depth audit, which can be an emotional and expensive experience.

2. *To pay less in taxes and keep more of the fruits of your labor.* This advantage is obvious, but it bears repeating. At first glance, a money market fund paying 13% interest may sound better than a municipal bond paying only a 10% yield. But when you consider the tax bite taken from your interest earnings, the tax-free municipal bond begins to look much more attractive. Of course, the final analysis depends on your own tax bracket, and the higher it is, the more tax-free investing makes sense. Another investment area that reduces your tax liability is *long-term capital gains* in traditional inflation hedges such as growth stocks, gold, silver, Swiss francs, real estate, etc. If held for more than one year, these are currently 60%

tax-free. Many of these investments allow you to defer taxes indefinitely as long as they are never sold.

3. *To engage in educational or charitable activities.* Public tax-exempt organizations can be established in the fields of education, religion, science, and charity—offering quite a variety of ways to use your money in an altruistic, as well as profitable, way. Public foundations can accumulate earnings and capital gains forever without paying any taxes, a fact wealthy Americans discovered early in this century. Another benefit is that many employees of public organizations do not have to pay social security and federal unemployment taxes.

ARE TAX EXEMPTIONS GOVERNMENT SUBSIDIES?

Before turning to specific how-to techniques in the world of tax exemptions, let me dismiss once and for all a bugaboo about tax-free living. Government bureaucrats are fond of referring to tax-free investing as "tax expenditures" or "government subsidies." They imply that there is little difference between a tax exemption and getting a subsidy check directly from the Treasury for your investment or business activities.

Nothing could be further from the truth. Does the thief who breaks in on a party and takes the jewelry from all the guests except one *subsidize* that person's wealth? Hardly. We cannot criticize a few individuals or institutions who are free from government levies—we can only wish that the "loopholes" of financial freedom were extended to *all* citizens.

Moreover, the idea that tax exemptions are actually "tax expenditures" implies that the government is the real owner of all citizens' wealth and income, and that it's up to the government to decide how much of it it will give to you. The truth, of course, is exactly the opposite. Individuals, not government, create wealth. It is government that forcibly takes it from the individual through myriad complicated levies. Therefore, the individual investor or businessman should not feel under any moral obligation to pay more than he is legally bound to pay. I hope this book will provide the techniques for you to escape a growing tax burden. Welcome to the exciting world of tax exemption!

THE TAX-FREE STRATEGY

Tax planning is more important than ever before. The tax burden is still very great in America. While the 1981–82 tax cuts attempted to provide relief, unfortunately, they have been replaced by sharply higher social security payments, increasing state and local taxes, and inflationary "bracket creep." The Feds can still take *up to 50%* of your income. These are the harsh realities of the 1980s!

The way to cut your taxes is to start planning now, before it's too late. But how? Overlooked personal deductions may not amount to much. And most tax shelters can be risky, illiquid, and costly. That's why more and more investors are turning to a whole new tax concept, which I call the "tax-free strategy."

This strategy is *not* a tax-protest measure or an illegal scheme. Rather, it is a powerful conceptual tool used by investors, businessmen, and executives to become legally *exempt* from federal, state, and social security taxes. This plan was originally developed for wealthy clients, but this book now makes it available to anyone—investors, businessmen, retirees, the self-employed, salaried workers, teachers, ministers, and expatriates. Consider the following cases, which are covered at length in the main text of the book.

Private Investor Earns Tax-Free Income

Using the tax-free strategy, you can earn *unlimited, nonreportable, tax-free* dividends as high as 15%. You can speculate in stocks, bonds, and money market funds, moving in and out of markets at will, while deferring your tax liability for as long as you wish. (See Chapters 2, 8, and 13.)

You can set up a "controlled" foreign corporation and trade in gold, strategic metals, and commodities on a tax-free basis. Or you can form an offshore investment company with a foreign partner and invest tax-free in virtually any market, including resort condominiums, high-yielding South African gold shares, commodity futures, and U.S. Treasury bills. (See Chapter 6.)

Family Business Earns $28,000 Tax-Free

A family business can earn $28,000 a year and completely avoid income taxes by taking advantage of the tax-free concept. Only *one* member of the family need pay into social security, while the rest of the family pays no federal taxes at all! A liberal pension program for all family members is a valuable fringe benefit. (See Chapter 3.)

Privately Held Corporation No Longer Pays Government

A closely held corporate business can completely eliminate its tax liabilities year after year by using the right strategy. This carefully conceived method permits the corporation to pay you a liberal salary while it avoids corporate income taxes entirely.

This is accomplished by establishing *several* trust accounts within the corporation, which are totally in your control. As your own trustee, you can invest in virtually anything, including gold. All interest, dividends, and capital gains accumulate tax-free. The amount of money you contribute to these trust accounts is virtually unlimited, and in many cases you can exceed your salary. This is indeed the ultimate tax shelter! (See Chapter 8.)

Americans Live Abroad Tax-Free

The new tax law greatly expands the exemptions for Americans living abroad. A working couple can earn *nearly $200,000* outside the United States and pay *no* federal, state, or social security taxes. Investment income is taxed starting at the *lowest* federal rates (12%) rather than the highest (50%) charged to at-home Americans. Overseas Americans can even avoid *foreign* levies by following a few simple rules. (See Chapter 5.)

If you know what to do, you can live and work tax-free *anywhere* in the world, including such high-tax areas as Europe, and still spend up to five weeks each year in the United States. Another technique allows you to spend up to six months in the United States while maintaining your tax-free, foreign-resident status. Even more liberal tax advantages apply to self-employed professionals working overseas.

Corporate Executives and Employees Get a Tax-Free Raise

It is possible to increase your compensation *by 30%* without you or your employer paying additional taxes. This technique also shows you how to get up to $100,000 in company stock at below-market prices without paying any taxes. And, starting this year, you can have your own tax-free investment program *outside* your corporate pension plan. By seeking new employment, corporate executives and employees can also eliminate social security and state income taxes. (See Chapters 4, 7, and 10.)

HOW THE WEALTHY AVOID TAXES

This book reveals how the wealthy have been using the tax-free strategy for years to avoid taxes. But more important, I have developed simple ways for you to use the same techniques to avoid taxes, no matter how much you make. Consider, for example:

Tax-Exempt Foundations

The rich have preserved their wealth for centuries through this technique. But you can set up your own tax-exempt foundation for as little as $100. Your own private foundation or public charity can accept tax-deductible donations from the general public. You can even *donate up to half your income* to your own foundation, and claim it as a deduction on your tax return. The foundation can invest its surplus funds in virtually any investment and earn tax-free interest, dividends, and capital gains. Your foundation is not subject to income, sales, or property taxes. The foundation's employees don't even have to pay social security or federal unemployment taxes. A tax-exempt organization qualifies for half-price postal rates on all its mail, as well. (See Chapter 9.)

How profitable can your foundation be? One tax-exempt organization recently reported over $200 million in annual revenues, $10 million in tax-free interest and dividends, and enough money to pay *cash* for a $30 million office building.

Tax Havens

Despite new restrictions in the U.S. tax law, the wealthy continue to use foreign corporations and trusts to avoid U.S. taxes. These techniques are perfectly legal, but are not widely circulated. This book reveals the details of these legitimate methods, and also warns you *against* phony schemes that rely primarily on secrecy laws in the Caribbean and Europe to protect you from the IRS. (See Chapter 6.)

Offshore tax planning can save you thousands of dollars every year, but you will have to use real professionals, not fly-by-night promoters. This book teaches you how to differentiate between them.

State Tax Havens

For years the big corporations have kept it a secret. But believe it or not, there are *seven* states inside the United States that have their own "tax-free strategy." If you are searching for a new job or for a place to retire, or if you want to relocate your business, read the chapter on *state tax havens.* You can save thousands by avoiding personal and corporate income taxes, sales taxes, and estate taxes. (See Chapter 10.)

Tax-Free Estate Planning

The wealthy have developed sophisticated techniques to keep their estates intact after death. For example, you can learn exactly how a millionaire businessman transferred $12.5 million to his heirs without paying a penny in federal estate or gift taxes. Also explained are the powerful advantages of stock recapitalization, private annuities, charitable and insurance trusts, creative gift-giving, and other little-known techniques that will eliminate death taxes. (See Chapter 11.)

TAX SHELTERS: HOW TO PROFIT FROM LONG-TERM CAPITAL GAINS

One very smart tax-saving device involves converting ordinary income into long-term capital gains. Income that you earn from your business or your investments is fully taxable, but if you can convert your income into long-term capital gains, 60% of the income becomes tax-exempt.

You can accomplish this through the wise use of tax shelters. This book highlights the tax shelters that promise the best long-term gains: real estate, cattle breeding, gold mining, and limited partnerships that are converted to public stock. (See Chapter 14.) You will also learn the following:

1. How to earn high tax-free interest on your checking account, bank certificates, utilities, and other stocks. (See Chapters 2 and 3.)
2. How to write off your child's college education. (See Chapter 3.)
3. How foreigners living in the United States avoid U.S. taxes. (See Chapter 3.)
4. How to beat social security taxes, *without losing* social security benefits. (See Chapter 7.)
5. How you can still put *gold* into your self-directed retirement plan! (See Chapter 8.)
6. How to set up your own self-directed Keogh, IRA, corporate pension, or teacher's annuity for only $10 a year, with no hidden fees. (See Chapter 8.)
7. How to recognize investments that could be a *disaster* in your retirement account. (See Chapter 8.)
8. How to avoid the sales tax, no matter where you live. (See Chapter 10.)

2

—Tax-Free Income: The Mystique of Municipal Bonds

THE STORY is told of an IRS agent assigned to audit a man who had claimed no taxable income for over ten years. As he drove up to the man's house, the agent noticed a Cadillac, an Italian sports car, and two Mercedes-Benzes in the open garage. A butler greeted the agent at the door of the Spanish-style mansion and showed him to the Olympic-size swimming pool, where the owner was relaxing after a heated game at his indoor tennis court. "I've caught this guy red-handed," the agent thought to himself, mentally smacking his lips.

But the IRS agent went away still hungry. True, this non-tax-payer was living in the lap of luxury, and true, the money had to come from somewhere. But it did not come from illegal dealings in the underground economy, as the IRS auditor had suspected. No, this man was living a luxurious *tax-free* life, thanks to the benefits of municipal bonds. Ten years before, he had inherited a small fortune from his grandfather and was now living quite comfortably on the tax-free interest paid by the municipal bonds he had purchased.

Of course, this is an unusual case. Not many of us have a rich grandfather, uncle, or other benefactor dying to give us a fortune. Most of us have to work for a living! And even if we did have a sudden windfall, investing it *all* in munies (as they are called in the trade) would be unsound. Inflation and rising interest rates have

28

been eating away at the profitability of municipal bonds over the past couple of decades.

When a bond is issued, it normally sells in $5,000 denominations at a "par" value of close to 100. (All bonds are priced on the basis of 100 points—above 100, the bond is said to be "above par," below 100, it is "below par.") Yield is determined by the currently prevailing interest rates. The investor loans his money to the state or local issuer for a long period of time, generally 20–30 years, receiving interest payments until the bond matures and the $5,000 is repaid.

When interest rates remain stable, bonds are a good investment. But when interest rates climb steadily, as they have done in recent years, the desirability of older bonds decreases. Why should a person tie up his money at 7–8% when he can buy a newly issued bond paying 12–15%? To balance this disparity, the price of the old bond falls, or is "discounted." An investor agrees to purchase an older, lower-yielding bond at a discounted price of say, 65, because he knows that it will reach 100 points when the bond matures. Thus, the low interest on his bond is compensated for by the capital gain he will receive.

For decades, long-term municipal bonds have suffered from low yields and falling prices. The trend of falling bond prices accelerated in the early 1980s, as interest rates hit all-time highs.

This brought about a unique situation in the early 1980s. For the first time, coupon yields on new state and local issues clearly exceeded the rise in cost of living in the United States. The following chart compares average long-term municipal bond yields with the Consumer Price Index over the past couple of decades.

As the chart demonstrates, yields on 20-year bonds climbed to 12% and higher in 1982, while the Consumer Price Index stayed under 8%. The net result was a superior *real* rate of return (after inflation) of about 4%. Moreover, the inordinately high level of interest rates in 1982 created an excellent opportunity for *capital gains* in the bond market once interest rates finally drifted downward.

The savvy investor can't dismiss the profit potential in the newly issued bonds. For example, a recent nuclear power plant bond issued by the Washington Public Power Supply System, a triple-A-rated bond issuer, paid an incredible 15% tax-free yield recently. Assuming an investor is in the 50% tax bracket, that's equivalent to a yield of 30% on taxable interest income! In addition, the investor

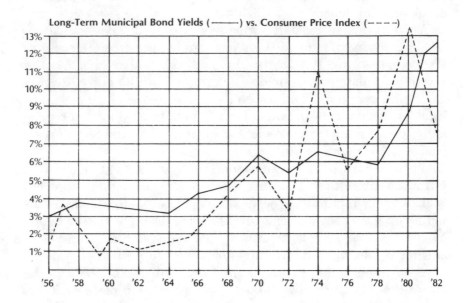

Long-Term Municipal Bond Yields (———) vs. Consumer Price Index (– – – –)

has the potential of making capital gains if interest rates come down temporarily. Finally, municipal bonds rated triple-A can be considered relatively safe when compared to other fixed-income securities. These bond investors will be clipping 15% coupons for many years, I suspect.

Clearly the time has come once again to investigate tax-free bonds! I'm not surprised that the municipal bond market has been growing rapidly in the past decade as inflation has pushed interest rates up. Today the municipal bond market exceeds $325 billion, $63 billion of which is owned by individuals.

But there are numerous pitfalls to watch for in this unique market, as outlined in this chapter.

WHY MUNICIPAL BONDS?

Of course, the most important reason investors are attracted to munies in the first place is their tax-free status. When the federal income tax was established in 1913, the law stated, "Interest upon obligations of a state, territory, or any political subdivision thereof is wholly exempt (excluded from gross income)." As far back as

1819 in *McCulloch vs. Maryland*, the Supreme Court ruled that states and the federal government cannot tax each other on their monetary instruments.

For this reason, state governments cannot tax the interest on U.S. Treasury securities, even though the *federal* government taxes the interest on its own securities. This is one reason why Treasury securities are popular—they are exempt from state and city taxation.

The tax-exempt status of municipal bonds becomes more attractive as your tax bracket moves to higher levels. Clearly, a foreigner living in a tax-haven country would have no desire to purchase munies, because their lower yield compares poorly to such income-producing investments as bonds, utilities, gold shares, money market funds, and Treasury bills. But an investor in the United States, faced with a government that takes up to 50% of his earnings, may find munies extremely attractive.

The following table shows the advantages of municipal bond yields based on your marginal tax bracket. This table is based on a husband and wife filing a joint return for 1982.

As the table clearly demonstrates, if you pay heavy federal income taxes, the tax-free yields on municipal bonds can beat the *after-tax* returns of many other investments. Suppose, for instance, that you invest $50,000 in a money market fund paying 15% annual interest. At the end of the year you will have earned $7,500. But if you are in the 50% tax bracket, the federal government will take $3,750, and your state and local governments could take a lot more, depending on where you live. Of the $7,500 you earned, you might keep a mere $3,000–$3,500. On the other hand, if you had pur-

Municipal Bond Yields and Your Tax Bracket

Net Joint Taxable Income	Federal Tax Bracket	Yield Necessary to Match 10% Municipal Bond
$20,200–$24,600	25%	13.3%
$24,600–$29,900	29%	14.1%
$29,900–$35,200	33%	14.9%
$35,200–$45,800	39%	16.4%
$45,800–$60,000	44%	17.9%
$60,000–$85,600	49%	19.6%
Over $85,600	50%	20.0%

chased a municipal bond yielding only 10%, you would have earned $5,000 free and clear, and it wouldn't even appear as income on your tax return! Thus, your actual yield would be 30–40% higher by purchasing municipal bonds.

Keep in mind, too, that many municipal bonds are returning yields higher than 10%, therefore magnifying their tax advantages.

All of the above analyses can be very misleading, however, unless you take your whole investment situation into account. Investors tend to forget that what we're talking about is *marginal* tax brackets, which are figured *after* you have taken all your deductions. Let me offer this illustration. Suppose you earned $100,000 in 1982. Clearly, you would be in the 50% bracket. But $100,000 is your *gross* income, *before* deductions. Let's say that your personal exemptions and deductions add up to $30,000. According to the chart, you're now in the 49% bracket. Moreover, if you did any financial planning in 1982, you would probably have invested heavily in *tax shelters* with high write-offs. Let's assume you have $25,000 in deductions from investing in some tax shelters. That brings your taxable income down to $45,000—which means you're in the 39% bracket. Finally, you decide to put 15% of your gross income into a Keogh pension plan, which gives you an additional $15,000 in deductions in 1982. Result? Your taxable income falls to $30,000, placing you ultimately in the 33% bracket.

The point I'm trying to make is that it's not your gross income that counts; what matters is your taxable income, after taking all your deductions for the year into account. If you're doing any tax planning at all, your deductions will be large, and your tax bracket will fall accordingly. Beware of investment counselors who say you're automatically in the 50% tax bracket when you earn more than $85,600!

Note, incidentally, that while tax shelters serve their purpose, there are many drawbacks when you get too heavily involved in them. High-write-off tax shelters are *risky* and *illiquid*, tying your money up for many years. You always need *ready income* for emergencies, new business and investment opportunities, and other unforeseeable circumstances. Municipal bonds serve that purpose, and should be considered as part of your investment portfolio. Don't be too heavily invested in munies, but you should consider them advantageous, especially when interest rates are peaking, or declining.

THE RISK OF INFLATION AND RISING INTEREST RATES

The major deterrent to buying municipal bonds, and particularly long-term bonds, is their vulnerability to high rates of inflation. Inflation has devastated the municipal bond market over the past decade. The state of Connecticut is a typical case. In the early 1970s—10 years ago—Connecticut issued a general obligation bond with a 5% coupon rate. The original price was approximately 100. Today that bond, which is due in 1992, is selling for 60¾. It has lost nearly 40% of its value because of rapidly rising inflation and interest rates over the past decade.

As long as inflation continues its upward climb, I don't recommend a "buy and hold" strategy for municipal bonds. There are still times when interest rates fall or are relatively stable—for example, 1975–76 and 1981–82. These are the best times to buy if you want to preserve your capital, and still earn high coupon rates.

When interest rates are peaking, I recommend buying new issues paying high dividends. Forget about the potential capital gains from buying discounted bonds and concentrate on long-term dividend yields; if you want speculative gains, there are better vehicles, such as corporate and Treasury bonds.

When interest rates are moving up again, stay only with short-term municipals, maturing in less than a year. Municipal money market funds are excellent vehicles.

THE RISK OF DEFAULT

How safe are municipal bonds? Many investors grow uneasy, worrying about the ability of local governments to repay their loan obligations during a time of high interest rates, high inflation, and the prospect of recession, which will cut heavily into their tax base. This concern has been highlighted by the recent default in 1975 of some New York City notes. The State of New York preferred to call it a "moratorium," or delay in payment for three years. At any rate, the moratorium was ruled unconstitutional. But bondholders have rightly been concerned about the financial health of the issuing government.

New York notes are not the only example of default. Many

lesser-known city governments have gone into bankruptcy. Revenue bonds, which depend on earnings from bridges, airports, utilities, etc. for repayment to bondholders, have faced default on occasion. During the Great Depression in the 1930s, many local governments were unable to pay their long-term obligations. However, almost all of these municipalities have since paid off their loans, or are in the process of paying them off.

There are several rating firms for municipal bonds. The best-known are Moody's and Standard & Poor's. If you want top-quality bonds, choose only bonds rated Aaa (Moody's rating) or AAA (S&P's rating). Many bond funds maintain a portfolio of high-quality issues. Bear in mind that high ratings are no guarantee that you'll never lose your money, or that a default is impossible. *Anything* is possible in this uncertain investment climate in which we live! But a high rating will help you limit your risks.

WHAT KINDS OF BONDS TO BUY

There are many different kinds of municipal bonds. Consequently, the risk of default varies not only according to the city or state of issue, but also according to the *type* of municipal bond you select.

General obligation issues are safer than revenue bonds. They are backed by the full faith and credit of the state or city, which can call upon the taxing power to pay its bills. Be aware, however, that governments are ultimately limited in how much revenue they can raise, as demonstrated by the passage of Proposition 13 in California.

Revenue issues are bonds issued to build service-producing facilities such as bridges, airports, and nuclear power plants. These bonds are repaid by exacting tolls and other "user fees." Ability to repay the bondholder depends on the earning power of the facility involved. Consequently, revenue bonds are more risky than general obligation bonds. Yields are traditionally higher, however, to counterbalance this additional risk. Most of these projects have proved successful and have paid out as promised, but you must take a careful look before investing.

Industrial bonds are even more risky, because a private company is involved with the local government in issuing the bonds. Here, the government makes a lease-back arrangement with a private company for the construction of convention centers, public golf courses, factories, campsites, industrial parks, pollution-control facilities, etc. Many of these projects have had to be subsidized because they turned out not to be profitable. But if you do your homework and find low-risk public projects, you should profit from higher yields without too much risk. There are many public enterprises that are extremely beneficial to local communities, and are worthy of your investment—whether it be an industrial park, a pollution-control system, a new airport, a baseball stadium, or a nuclear power plant. Contrast these tax-free municipal issues to *taxable* federal bonds that frequently result in counterproductive or unethical activities over which you have no control!

If you're interested in an industrial bond, be sure to investigate the security of the private company and its net worth, as well as the solvency of the town that issued the bonds.

Avoid "moral obligation" bonds issued by New York State and other local governments. These have no more legal backing than a "gentleman's agreement." If a default occurs, the state legislature might not agree to pay, even though the governor or administration says the state is morally obligated.

Callable bonds can be called in by the issuer prior to maturity. If interest rates fall and a municipality finds that it is paying more than the current interest rates, it will pay off the entire debt and issue new bonds at the lower interest rates. Callable bonds are difficult to avoid, and you should simply accept them as a fact of life.

There have been some genuine innovations in this field recently. Some states now issue short-term notes, coming due in 5 years or less rather than the traditional 20–30 years. Others are even more creative, offering "variable-rate" municipal bonds, for which the principal or face value remains constant, but the return fluctuates with national interest rates. Still others promise to redeem their bonds at par after a few years. In essence, these municipal issuers are seeking to take some of the risk out of buying munies in order to make their bonds more marketable.

MUNICIPAL BOND INSURANCE

You can buy municipal bonds that are insured by the Municipal Bond Insurance Association (MBIA). This insurance company, a subsidiary of Aetna, Fireman's Fund, Travelers, and Continental insurance companies, guarantees payment of principal and interest on qualified issues. Standard & Poor's gives a triple-A rating to all MBIA-insured bonds. Naturally the yield on insured bonds is less than on those without insurance. For details, write:

Municipal Issuers Service Corporation
34 South Broadway
P.O. Box 788
White Plains, NY 10602
Telephone 914-946-4242

Ask for the pamphlet "Insured Municipal Bonds: Triple-A Protection for Investors."

HOW TO BUY MUNICIPAL BONDS: THREE CHOICES

Brokers and money managers make it extremely convenient to buy and sell municipal bonds. Several dealers specialize in state and local bond issues, while others have established unit trusts and mutual funds to trade them. Retirees or others who want monthly income have several alternatives available to them.

Buying Bonds Through a Broker

The most traditional way to buy tax-free bonds is to buy individual issues through a reputable broker. This has several advantages.

First, you maintain a high degree of *financial privacy*. The bonds are typically serialized and in bearer form, although the 1982 tax reform measure requires new bonds to be registered. Bearer bonds have an added security risk, however, because whoever holds the bonds is considered the legal owner, and can sell them for cash. Therefore, you should store your bonds in a secure location, such as a safety deposit box or private vault. It would also be wise to keep a separate listing of the serial numbers of the bonds in case they are stolen. Each bond will have *coupons* attached to it. These coupons are clipped every six months, taken to the bank, and deposited or cashed. It's that simple!

Your privacy is further enhanced by the fact that under current law, the ownership of municipal bonds does not have to be reported on your federal income tax form. This is because interest you earn from clipping coupons is completely exempt from federal income taxes. IRS auditors do ask the question, "Did you earn any tax-free income during the year?" If you answer yes, they may try to disallow interest deductions if you borrowed money for investment purposes. But the question isn't asked on your income tax form, so unless you are audited you won't have to reveal your ownership of them.

If you want to avoid state and local income taxes as well, you have to purchase municipal bonds issued only within your state or city. For example, if you lived in a high-tax state such as New York, you could have a "double tax exemption" by limiting your municipal bond selection to New York State issues. Similarly, if you live in New York City, you could have a "triple tax exemption" by purchasing only New York City notes and bonds. Bond issues are sufficiently numerous in most states to give you a wide selection.

Of course, limiting yourself to the state or local issues in your area does have its drawbacks. It may cause you to violate a cardinal principle of investing, which is to diversify to spread your risk. It is possible to purchase municipal bonds from other jurisdictions in the United States that would still be tax-exempt in your state (such as bonds from Puerto Rico or the District of Columbia), but this has limited application.

When choosing a municipal issue, there are two variables to consider: dividend yield and capital appreciation. If you are more interested in the latter, you could buy low-yield bonds at a heavy discount. For example, a bond that was issued a decade or two ago at a very low interest rate might be purchased for 50 points today. The dividend yield would not keep up with inflation, but at maturity the bond would be worth 100, or close to it, doubling your investment. If you want a combination of higher yields and capital appreciation, you could purchase fairly recent issues that have since fallen in price because of even higher interest rates. But my recommendation is that you stress the highest yields possible, without taking undue risk. This generally means buying new bonds at or near par (100), with yields in the range of 12–15%. Don't plan on holding these bonds forever. Sell them when it appears that interest rates are going to climb steeply. Remember, your goal should be high tax-free earnings, not capital appreciation (or capital losses). As I stated earlier, I feel that there are better investment media than municipal bonds for capital appreciation.

How to sell? Don't be misled by stockbrokers who tell you that there is no secondary market in municipals. It is true that *most* issues are held to maturity by the original purchaser, and that there is no central exchange for munies. But there is still sufficient trading to provide a market for your bonds. When you sell your bonds through a major bond broker, your issue will be placed on the dealers' "blue list" along with hundreds of other bonds currently for sale. Some brokers will give you a firm bid over the telephone, if you bought the issue from them, but normally it takes some time to sell your bond. How much time depends on market conditions and national interest rates. The bid/ask spread is always in fluctuation, and you can usually expect to pay 2–4% commissions.

Most municipal bonds are sold in lots of $5,000 or more, although some brokerage firms will offer them in lots of $1,000. Frankly, I don't recommend the purchase of *individual* munies unless you're investing $25,000 or more.

All major brokerage houses (Merrill Lynch, Dean Witter, Bache, etc.) have municipal bond departments. In addition, some brokerage firms specialize exclusively in municipal bonds. One such firm is:

Lebenthal & Co. Inc.
One State Street Plaza
New York, NY 10004
Toll-free 800-221-5822
In New York, 212-425-6116 (collect)

Closed-End Unit Investment Trusts

Investment trusts in municipal bonds were created by brokerage firms as a convenient and inexpensive way for high-income and retired people to get a *monthly tax-free income*. These trusts are aimed at paying a high yield, recently as high as 12–13% annual interest. The sponsor buys a pool of municipal bonds, and sells them to investors at $1,000 a unit. A commission or "load" fee of about 4–4½% is normally charged. Once all the units are sold, the trust becomes a "closed" fund, and no further units are issued. The investor receives a monthly check, or, if he prefers, he can have the interest reinvested. There is no penalty for withdrawing principal, although units will be sold at the going market price and if interest rates have risen, the unit price will have fallen. There is no fee for selling, and administrative expenses are very low. Any capital gains on the trust units would be taxable at normal capital-gains rates.

There are a few unit trusts in New York, Pennsylvania, and other large states that invest only in local issues to avoid federal, state, and local taxes, thus producing a "triple exemption." Of course, investors from other states have to pay their state and local income taxes.

Unit trusts in municipal bonds are underwritten by many major brokerage firms. Two investment firms that specialize in unit investments trusts are:

Kemper Tax-Exempt Income Trust Series
120 South LaSalle St.
Chicago, IL 60603
Toll-free 800-621-1048
In Illinois, 312-845-1892

Nuveen Tax-Exempt Bond Fund Series
61 Broadway
New York, NY 10006
212-668-9500

The Kemper series are issued every month. As quickly as one unit trust is closed, another one is opened. Kemper also offers a "load" (commissioned) municipal bond fund that is always available for new investors.

The Nuveen series are issued more frequently, typically twice a month. They also offer single-state series from time to time, so that investors can avoid state taxes as well as federal. Nuveen has issued tax-exempt funds for California, New York, Pennsylvania, Michigan, Minnesota, and Massachusetts. Nuveen also has a municipal money market fund, but the minimum investment is $25,000.

All major brokerage firms underwrite Kemper and Nuveen offerings, if you prefer working with a local broker.

Tax-Free No-Load Municipal Bond Funds

The latest innovation in the field of municipals is the creation of "no-load" (no commission, no broker) mutual funds that specialize in municipal bonds and then pass the tax-free savings on to customers. These no-load bond funds have been extremely popular, and the number of new funds is increasing monthly. All the major mutual fund leaders offer them (Dreyfus, Fidelity, Scudder, Vanguard, Rowe Price, etc.).

The advantages are clear. You get diversification and professional management without the hassles of coupon-clipping, selection of bonds, pressure from brokers, etc. In addition, you pay no up-front commissions, so 100% of your money goes to work for you. There is neither a charge nor a waiting period for withdrawing your money, as there would be if you traded municipal bonds directly through a broker. In fact, many mutual fund organizations permit you to withdraw your money by check. The net asset value of each fund is listed under "mutual funds" in the *Wall Street Journal* or your local newspaper, so the value of your investment can be determined easily.

All of these services come at a cost, of course. There is a management fee, usually less than 1% annually, that slightly reduces your net asset value. And, like any portfolio of municipal bonds, the fund will lose value if interest rates climb. Conversely, if interest rates fall, your fund will increase in value. But the overall savings on commissions are significant when you buy into a no-load fund.

During the Dollar Boom of 1980–81, when interest rates skyrocketed to the 20% level, most municipal bond funds lost 30% of their value or more. But average yields also hit all-time highs, reaching 12–13% in 1982! To avoid the disastrous plunge in capital during a spike in interest rates, several fund managers created short-term "money market" funds in municipal bonds. These funds maintained a short, less-than-100-day maturity in order to avoid capital losses. It was a good place for the tax-free investor to place his money during a credit squeeze, and yields still reached a respectable 7–8% in 1982.

Vanguard is the leader in offering the widest variety of municipal bond funds, with a choice of five:

Vanguard's Municipal Bond Funds		
Fund	Recent Yield	Average Maturity of Bonds
Money market	7.38%	77 days
Short-term	7.77%	256 days
Intermediate	9.25%	9.7 years
Long-term	10.38%	22.9 years
High-yield	10.99%	24.2 years

Minimum investment in Vanguard's funds is $3,000. Vanguard offers a check-writing privilege on all five funds, plus a "telephone switch" privilege using its 800 number, so you can switch from one municipal bond fund to any other Vanguard fund, just by calling on the telephone. For details, write or call:

Vanguard Municipal Bond Funds
P.O. Box 2600
Valley Forge, PA 19482
Toll-free 800-523-7910
In Pennsylvania, 800-362-7688

There are almost 50 other tax-free funds available, so you might wish to check the following municipal bond funds:

Long-Term Municipal Bond Funds

Name of Fund	Minimum Investment	Check-Writing Privilege?
Dreyfus Tax Exempt Bond Fund 767 Fifth Ave. New York, NY 10022 800-223-5525 In N.Y., 212-935-6633 collect	$2,500	No
Fidelity Municipal Bond Fund 82 Devonshire Sq. Boston, MA 02109 Toll-free 800-225-6190 In Mass., 617-726-0650	$2,500	No
Nuveen Municipal Bond Fund 230 W. Monroe St. Chicago, IL 60606 312-782-2655	$5,000	No
Rowe Price Tax-Free Income Fund 100 East Pratt St. Baltimore, MD 21202 800-638-5660 In Md., 301-547-2308	$1,000	Yes
Scudder Managed Municipal Bonds 175 Federal St. Boston, MA 02110 800-225-2470 In Mass., 617-482-3990	$1,000	No

Money Market Municipal Bond Funds

Name of Fund	Minimum Investment	Check-Writing Privilege?
Dreyfus Tax Exempt Money Market Fund P. O. Box 600 Middlesex, NJ 08846 800-345-8501 In Pa., 800-662-5180	$5,000	Yes
Fidelity Tax-Exempt Money Market Trust 82 Devonshire Sq. Boston, MA 02109 Toll-free 800-225-6190 In Mass., 617-726-0650	$20,000	No
Nuveen Tax-Exempt Bond Fund 230 W. Monroe St. Chicago, IL 60606 800-621-2431 In Ill., 312-621-3264	$25,000	No
Rowe Price Tax-Exempt Money Fund 100 East Pratt St. Baltimore, MD 21202 800-638-5660 In Md., 301-547-2308	$1,000	Yes
Scudder Tax-Free Money Fund 175 Federal St. Boston, MA 02110 800-225-2470 In Mass., 617-482-3990	$1,000	Yes

ARE MUNICIPAL BONDS FOR YOU?

The financial markets have created easy ways to invest in municipal bonds. You have your choice of investing in the bonds themselves, in unit trusts, or in mutual funds. Privacy and tax-free income make municipal bonds extremely attractive, even if they don't yield as much as taxable investments. Your principal can be in jeopardy, however—so be careful how and when you buy. The best time to buy munies is when interest rates are peaking, or declining. Take advantage of high coupon yields. Don't plan to hold on forever—there's a time to buy and a time to sell. If interest rates suddenly increase, switch out of long-term bonds and into money market funds for safety and preservation of principal. Diversify to spread your risk. Don't depend exclusively on municipal bonds for financial independence. Consider them as one of many worthwhile investments, including growth stocks, precious metals, tax-sheltered limited partnerships, real estate, collectibles, foreign currencies, and money market funds.

Several years ago there was a news report of a wealthy widow who was receiving over $10 million annually in tax-free income. She had not filed a federal income tax return for years. Certainly she had maintained her financial privacy (that is, until some reporter found out about her unique situation). But she could have done much more with her money if she had protected herself from tremendous losses in the value of her bonds because of destructive inflationary forces over the past decade or two. If she had diversified most of her estate in long-term capital assets while still keeping a *small portion* of her estate tied up in municipal bonds for living expenses, she would undoubtedly have paid a few thousand dollars in taxes each year, but her overall after-tax profits could have been substantially more than $10 million. Though the figures may be lower in your personal situation, the principle is still the same.

Problem Solver #1

Q. We are a retired couple who depend on our stocks and bonds to supplement social security. But half of every bit of interest and dividends goes to the government! What can we do?

A. You have several alternatives. This chapter outlines the incredible tax-free benefits of municipal bonds. When interest rates are steady or falling, consider selling your stocks and bonds and switching to high-quality munies or a municipal bond fund. There are two immediate benefits. First, you will undoubtedly earn more income because even the best of blue-chip stocks pay only modest dividends. Second, your income from munies would be entirely free of federal income taxes.

If inflation and interest rates start climbing, consider switching out of long-term municipal bonds, and into a tax-free money market fund. Although your income level will drop, you will preserve your capital.

There are, of course, other alternatives that you should consider, such as tax-deferred annuities, tax shelters, and growth stocks that earn long-term capital gains. These will be discussed in future chapters.

3

—Tax-Free Income: From Utilities to Insurance

MUNICIPAL BONDS are probably the only *unlimited* source of tax-exempt income. A wealthy investor could earn millions of dollars in tax-free municipal bonds if he wanted to—the only limit is that imposed by the investor himself. There are numerous other techniques available to those seeking high tax-free income, but these are usually limited in one way or another. Nevertheless, you can earn a great deal of income completely exempt from federal taxation by taking advantage of many of these tax-free investment vehicles.

A few sources of tax-free income include return-of-capital dividends on utilities and real estate investment trusts (REITs); income while employed abroad; insurance proceeds; awards and scholarships; personal exemptions for individual family members; and income-splitting techniques. Let's examine the advantages and disadvantages of each of these methods.

ALL-SAVERS CERTIFICATES

The Economic Recovery Act of 1981 created a substantial unprecedented tax shelter for interest paid on bank deposits. By purchasing an All-Savers Certificate at a local bank or savings institution, investors could earn up to $1,000 on a single return or $2,000 on a joint return without owing any tax. The yield on All-Savers Certificates was equal to 70% of the annual yield on 52-week Treasury notes. The rate changed every 4 weeks, when a new auction for the Treasury notes took place.

When the All-Savers Certificates were first issued, interest rates were at extremely high levels in the United States, and the annual yield was quite advantageous at 12.6%. Normally interest rates do not exceed the inflation rate, but during 1981–82, the real rate of interest (*after* inflation) reached dramatic positive levels of 10% or more. This was a unique situation created by the Federal Reserve's tight monetary policy in the early 1980s, and could not last forever.

At any rate, high-income taxpayers still had to look to other sources of tax-free income because of the $2,000 limitation on All-Savers Certificates. Unfortunately, All-Savers Certificates were discontinued in 1982.

Frankly, I believe that *all* interest, dividends, and capital gains should be exempt from income taxation in order to promote capital expansion in the United States. But that day is far from coming, I'm afraid.

RETURN-OF-CAPITAL UTILITIES

From time to time, some utility companies face heavy costs because of new construction, depreciation, fuel costs, or changing weather conditions. As a result, these utility companies do not accumulate any retained earnings during the year, and therefore cannot pay a true dividend to their shareholders. Instead, the annual payment is treated as a "return of capital" rather than as a profit, and is free from *current* federal income taxes. This actually is not so much a tax exemption as it is a tax *deferral.* The income is not currently taxed, but the "cost basis" of your utility stock is reduced by the amount of the return-of-capital dividend, so that when you eventually sell the stock, your capital gains are higher. In essence, if you hold the stock for more than a year, your dividend income becomes a *long-term capital gain.*

For example, suppose you bought a utility stock for $20 a share. This year the company pays a $2 return-of-capital dividend. This dividend reduces the cost basis of your stock to $18. Let's suppose that in a year, the stock appreciates in value to $25, and you decide to sell. Your capital gain is $7 ($25 minus $18). If you held for more than a year, it's 60% tax-free. As you can see, while the utility income isn't exactly "tax-exempt," you do get tax-free use of the income as long as you own the stock, and when you sell, a full 60% of the income remains tax-free.

The main problem facing investors who want return-of-capital income lies in determining which utilities will pay tax-free dividends in the future, and, more importantly, *why.* Obviously, no company wants to have an unprofitable year, but there are often legitimate reasons for temporarily not declaring a profit. In the past few years, the following companies have paid tax-free dividends at 13–15% yields: Cleveland Electric, Long Island Lighting, New York State Electric and Gas, Pennsylvania Power & Light, Virginia Electric and Power, and Public Service Co. of New Hampshire.

There are brokerage firms that specialize in predicting which utility companies are expected to pay out "very high" tax-free dividends. One such brokerage firm is:

Kidder-Peabody & Co.
Three Girard Plaza
Philadelphia, PA 19102
Telephone 215-496-2000

Ask for information on "Electric Utilities Return of Capital Dividends."

Unlike municipal bonds, return-of-capital dividends must be reported on Schedule B of your tax return, even though the dividends are currently tax-free.

In addition to earning tax-free return-of-capital dividends, many utilities qualify for tax-deferred dividends. Under current law, you can earn up to $750 or $1,500 per couple in dividends from qualified utility stock without paying current taxes. However, when you sell the utility stock, your cost basis is reduced by the tax-free earnings. In essence, you get long-term capital gains on the earnings when you sell.

OTHER SOURCES OF RETURN-OF-CAPITAL INCOME

Utilities are not the only stocks that pay return-of-capital dividends. In fact, a great many companies declare non-profit dividends from time to time.

Real estate investment trusts (*REITs*), in particular, have declared considerable return-of-capital dividends. A recent study by the National Association of Real Estate Investment Trusts shows that out of the 110 REITs it monitored, over 50 paid dividends as either return-of-capital, long-term gains, or both. Last year, four REITs paid 100% of their dividends in tax-free return-of-capital distributions.

A REIT is a trust that invests in several pieces of property for maximum diversification. Shares of the trust are sold to the public. Frequently the depreciation and other write-offs associated with the properties will be greater than their amortization schedules, resulting in a new cash flow that is higher than their reported earnings. As a result, dividends are considered "return of capital," rather than income-produced profits. Many REITs also engage in high construction costs at certain times, which result in return-of-capital earnings. When properties are sold, the REIT declares a dividend which is partially or wholly treated as a 60%-tax-free long-term gain.

Annual yields on REITs vary greatly, from 3% to 14%. Recently, the average return of all REITs has been approximately 7%, clearly below the rates of most tax-exempt investments. General Growth Properties, a large equity-type REIT traded on the New York Stock Exchange and one that frequently pays return-of-capital dividends, typically pays only 5–6% annual dividends. Most REIT investors are looking for capital appreciation more than high dividends.

My recommendation, therefore, is that you *not* purchase REITs if you are looking primarily for a source of steady high income. However, REITs do provide a good way to spread your risk when speculating in the volatile commercial real estate markets. During a real estate boom, commercial property such as hotels, shopping centers, and office buildings could skyrocket in value, pushing up the value of your real estate stocks. But beware of the real estate bust as well! In the early 1970s, REITs were the darlings of most brokerage houses and reached record-breaking prices in 1973–74. But when commercial real estate took a nose dive, the REITs collapsed. They made a determined attempt to recover in the late 1970s, but were turned back again by the real estate bear market in the early 1980s. They have not yet recovered to their 1973–74 highs. If another boom hits real estate in the 1980s, trading in REITs may be one of the most convenient and profitable ways to take advantage of it, without having to incur a huge personal debt.

Before you consider real estate stock, I recommend that you read the *REIT Fact Book*, available for $5 from the National Association of Real Estate Investment Trusts, 1101 17th St. NW, Washington, DC 20036. The association will also send you a list of REITs currently on the market. Several major brokerage houses have REIT specialists and issue reports from time to time (check with Merrill Lynch, for example).

Remember that return-of-capital dividends aren't entirely tax-free, as I mentioned in the utilities section. The amount of the dividend is subtracted from the cost basis of the price you paid for the REIT, so that when you sell your stocks, 40% of the dividend is taxed as a long-term capital gain.

INCOME SPLITTING: TAKING ADVANTAGE OF PERSONAL EXEMPTIONS

Another major category for tax-free income may seem simplistic, but through careful planning it can be extremely valuable as a tax-saving tool. As you are aware, every taxpayer is entitled to at least one personal "exemption" of $1,000. Those over 65 are entitled to another exemption of $1,000. Blind taxpayers receive still another $1,000 exemption. You can also claim $1,000 for each of your children you support as long as they are under 19 years of age or students, no matter how much they earn.

In addition, each taxpayer is entitled to an earned-income exclusion, below which he is not subject to federal income taxes. This so-called zero bracket amount (formerly the standard deduction) varies with the status of taxpayers. Single taxpayers get a ZBA of $2,300, while married couples filing jointly get a total ZBA of $3,400.

For instance:

— A single worker could earn up to $3,300 without paying federal income taxes ($1,000 personal exemption plus $2,300 ZBA).
— A retired couple over 65 years old could have combined earnings of $7,400 without incurring federal income taxes.
— A family of five could earn *over $18,000* and not pay a single penny in federal taxes if they are involved in a family business.

TAX-FREE FAMILY BUSINESS

Let's see how it would be possible for a family of five to earn over $18,000 tax-free. First, the parents file a joint return, claiming personal exemptions of $5,000, or $1,000 for each family member. They also claim a zero bracket amount of $3,400. This totals $8,400 of tax-free earnings. In addition, the three children could *each* earn $2,300 working in the family business. As a bonus, the children can earn an additional $1,000 in interest or other unearned income and claim their own $1,000 personal exemption against it. This essentially becomes a double personal exemption, once on the parents' return and again on the child's return. Total tax-free income: $18,300!

It's also possible to earn an additional family income of $10,000 and not pay any income taxes, by setting up an individual retirement account (IRA) for each member of the family. The new law allows each worker to place up to $2,000 in earned income into an IRA each year. Thus, if the husband and wife earned $17,400, and each child earned $4,300, each person could make a maximum contribution of $2,000 in an IRA. *Total tax-free family income could thus reach $28,300!*

Note, however, that this analysis is based on some unusual assumptions. First, each of the three children must be working in a family business or other enterprise. Second, they would each need to have separate savings accounts that earn each of them $1,000. That assumes a capital investment of nearly $10,000 per child. Third, if each has an IRA, it assumes a high rate of savings by the family. To take full advantage of this kind of situation would, of course, require considerable *tax planning*.

Most families would be limited to $8,400 in tax-free earnings because their children aren't working and don't have sizable savings accounts. Admittedly, $8,400 is hardly enough for a family of five to live on!

Nevertheless, this illustration demonstrates the advantages of income splitting, or having all members of the family earn income instead of just the parents. This concept is particularly useful when it comes to interest, dividends, and capital gains on savings or investments. Suppose, for example, that this year you earn $5,000 in dividends from a money market fund, and that you're in the 30% bracket. On April 15, you will owe the federal government $1,500 from the dividends you earned. On the other hand, if the money market dividends had been earned by your daughter, she would have paid only about $600 in income taxes because she would be in a much lower tax bracket. Thus, you can see how advantageous income splitting is as a tax-planning tool. This is particularly useful for money earmarked for college funds, or for other child-related expenses.

Parents may each give up to $10,000 in stocks, bonds, money, or other investments to their children without incurring a gift tax (which begins at 20 percent in excess of $10,000 and can increase as much as 50 to 70 percent under certain circumstances). Interest or dividends earned from the gifts are then taxable at the children's marginal bracket, which can amount to a sizable savings.

Capital assets, such as growth stocks or gold coins, can also be given, so that when the investment is sold, the profit is taxed at lower rates.

The Uniform Gift to Minors Act makes it simple to give money to your children, even if they are under legal age. Mutual funds, in particular, are an easy way to assign money to your children for dividends or capital gains. But remember that once you give money or assets to your children, you cannot get it back. Unless you take steps in advance to retain some control, it will be legally owned by them, and you'll have no legal control over what they do with the money.

The financial advantages are clear, but many parents are reluctant to hand over large amounts of money or assets to their children on a silver platter. This is the biggest drawback to income-splitting techniques.

TEN-YEAR TRUSTS AND INTEREST-FREE LOANS

There are ways around this sticky problem, however. One method is to *lend* the money to your children instead of giving it to them. There are several techniques for doing this. One is called the *10-year Clifford trust*. This trust, set up by your attorney, is funded by you on behalf of your children. Any earnings from the trust are taxed to your children, who should be in a much lower tax bracket. After 10 years, the money reverts to you. Meanwhile, the earnings can be used by your children for practically any purpose—such as school tuition, books, or entertainment.

A simpler approach that has recently gained popularity is the use of *interest-free loans.* The trust concept can be expensive and requires annual tax reports, but an interest-free loan to your child can be convenient and less costly. A trust should be set up to handle the interest-free loans for minors, but to maintain privacy and simplicity you might prefer a less formal agreement. Under this arrangement, you prepare a promissory note, *payable on demand,* at no interest, and lend the money to your child. Your child then opens a savings account, money market fund, or other interest-bearing instrument, and earns interest or dividends. He won't even have to file a tax return if the earnings don't exceed $1,000. He can use the earnings for practically any purpose without jeopardizing your ability to claim him as a dependent, as long as he does not contribute to such "support" items as food, housing, clothing, etc. He can use the money to purchase a used car, pay for college expenses, finance a summer trip, etc. The main advantage of the demand note is that if you don't approve of how he spends the money, you can always demand that the principal be returned immediately.

Another advantage is that the use of interest-free loans is a private, low-profile tax shelter that does not show up on your tax return. There are no reporting requirements as there are for trusts. When the IRS has found out about interest-free loans, it has tried to argue in court that the interest earned from these loans is a gift, and is therefore taxable to the lender. But the courts have ruled time and time again in favor of the taxpayers.

The best book on the subject is called *Tax Savings Through Interest-Free Loans,* by Harry G. Gordon, Attorney at Law, 722 Coleridge Dr., Greensboro, NC 27410 ($14.95 plus $2 for postage and handling). The book is a 150-page manual containing step-by-step instructions, sample demand notes, investment strategies, support rules, and sample trusts. A second book by Gordon is entitled *More on Interest-Free Loans* ($14.95, same address), which details corporate interest-free loans, loans to minors without a trust, record-keeping requirements, and IRS rulings. Highly recommended!

OTHER SOURCES OF TAX-FREE INCOME

So far we have discussed sources of tax-free income in the form of interest and dividends. But there are several other important categories of tax-free income that do not involve the investment field.

Some of these may not apply to your current situation, but you should still be aware of them.

Prizes, Awards, and Fellowships

Several types of awards are given every year to scientists, writers, and public figures. The Nobel and the Pulitzer prizes are two prominent examples. Surprisingly, the income from these awards is completely tax-free to the recipients! Of course, not too many of us can qualify for a $180,000 Nobel Prize, but there are an amazing number of other prizes, awards, and scholarships for which we or our children may qualify.

Cash awards from a public foundation, in recognition of scientific, educational, religious, or charitable achievements, are completely nontaxable to the award winner. There are thousands of awards given every year for outstanding public achievements.

One of the key factors used in deciding whether a prize or award is exempt is whether you entered a contest or promoted yourself in achieving the award or prize. Prizes won on a television or radio program are taxable at their "fair market value" because the contestants entered the program and therefore actively sought the award. The same principle applies to lotteries, sweepstakes, and other contests.

But in the case of major achievement awards such as the Nobel Prize, candidates' names are entered by fellow scientists, writers, or other professionals, and not by the individual himself. Thus, they are tax-free.

Scholarships to colleges, universities, and technical schools are not considered taxable income in most cases. As long as you are seeking a college degree, income from such prestigious awards as the Rhodes and Fulbright scholarships is tax-free. This includes room and board, tuition, books, and family allowances. Income you earn from teaching is also exempt if it is required as part of the college degree. If teaching is not considered a requirement for a degree, but is treated as a service rendered for the university or foundation, the income from the scholarship is taxable.

Fellowship awards for non-degree-seeking candidates are also tax-free, but only up to $300 a month for 36 months. After that, the funds are taxable. Travel and related expenses are not treated as part of the $300-a-month limitation, and are tax-free.

Nontaxable grants include fellowships and scholarships offered by the National Institute of Health, National Science Foundation, and the National Research Service Awards, as well as numerous smaller foundations.

You can personally offer tax-free grants, scholarships, or awards to individuals through your favorite university, church, or charitable organization, or through your own public foundation. The award must follow the stringent requirements imposed on all exemplary awards and student scholarships, however. This is not an opportunity for foundation directors to award scholarships to their own children!

Gifts and Inheritances

Gifts are not taxable to the receiver as long as no service or benefits are expected in return for the gift. This is fairly straightforward when applied to family members or relatives.

However, gifts between business associates are more debatable, because it is often difficult to prove motivation. If Mr. Smith gives Mr. Jones a Rolex watch, and Mr. Jones gives Mr. Smith season football tickets, neither recipient must pay taxes on his gift, unless it can be proved that one gift would not have been given without the other. Both businessmen must demonstrate that neither one expected remuneration in return, and that each acted solely out of his unselfish friendship with the other.

Inherited property or cash is not normally taxable as income unless, again, there is indication that the inheritance was in payment for past or future services. Often a close friendship develops between an individual and his lawyer, doctor, or other professional or executive, and he leaves something to the professional in his will. This is a true gift and should not be taxed as income. If, for example, a man leaves $10,000 to his attorney as a token of his appreciation for kindness shown to the family, the money would be tax-free. But if the $10,000 actually represented payment for some *specific* past or future services, it would be taxable as income to the attorney.

Executor's fees for administering an estate can be considered a tax-free "legacy" if the will states that the executor will receive the fees whether he agrees to act as executor or not.

Insurance Proceeds

Life insurance proceeds are normally free of income taxes if the beneficiary was related to the deceased. On the other hand, if you own a policy on someone not related to you, it is called a "wagering agreement," and the proceeds are taxable.

Lawsuits

As Americans become more and more suit-happy, the chances are increasing that you will someday become involved in a lawsuit. Let's hope you win! Proceeds from some kinds of lawsuits are free from income taxes. In particular, you do not have to declare funds received from a suit involving personal injury claims, including slander and libel. However, money received as a result of injuries to your "business reputation" or loss of profits would be considered taxable income. Consequently, in many business cases, claimants sue for loss of profits *and* loss of property, since the latter would be exempt from taxes, as long as the compensation does not exceed the actual cost of the property.

Alimony and Child Support

In divorce cases, alimony is almost always taxable to the wife and deductible to the husband. Child support, however, can be tax-exempt if it is set up properly. The key here is to keep the amount paid for the children's support separate from the wife's alimony. If no distinction is made, the IRS assumes that all payments represent alimony, which is fully taxable. Child support is described as payments for the support of any children under the age of 21.

Property settlements and lump-sum payments from a divorce are also treated as tax-free income in most cases.

Cash Rebates

Cash rebates are becoming more and more popular all the time as a way for manufacturers to reduce a big inventory of cars, trucks, appliances, and equipment. When the cash rebate comes directly from the manufacturer, it is really nothing more than a discount or price reduction on the item you bought, and therefore is not taxable income.

Foreign Ambassadors and Diplomats

Ambassadors and diplomats of foreign governments enjoy many privileges in the United States. Diplomatic immunity from civil lawsuits is just one advantage. Another important benefit is that they are not required to pay any U.S. income taxes. In addition, they are exempt from social security, unemployment taxes, and even sales taxes. The secret, then, is for you to leave the U.S. and become an expatriate, then become a citizen of a tax haven, and return to the United States as a foreign diplomat! That way you can live tax-free and still enjoy the great life in the States!

Rental Income

Strangely enough, a peculiar section of the U.S. Tax Code allows you to exclude up to two weeks of rental income on investment property you own. In other words, if you own a condominium or other investment property and rent it out for only two weeks of the year, you can exclude the income from your tax return.

Consequently, you could rent your beachfront condo for a couple of weeks during the high-priced season and pocket several thousand dollars. Then use the condo personally for the rest of the year. Or you could buy a time-sharing investment in a resort condominium for two weeks, and then rent it out for tax-free income. An ingenious loophole!

The one drawback to this two-week exemption is that you cannot take the normal write-offs, such as depreciation, on your investment real estate.

THE WIDE WORLD OF TAX-FREE INCOME AND INVESTING

I've highlighted some of the more interesting sources of tax-exempt income. The most complete listing is found in J. K. Lasser's *Your Income Tax* (Simon & Schuster, 1230 Ave. of the Americas, New York, NY 10020; $5.95). This book is not tax-free, but it is tax-deductible!

In this chapter, I've demonstrated the wide variety of investments and sources of income that are completely or partially exempt from government taxation. Whether you have a family business, invest in a bank certificate or utilities, make interest-free loans to your children, receive an inheritance from your grandparents, or win a scholarship, you now know the tremendous benefits of tax-free living.

Problem Solver #2

Q. Is there any way I can get a tax deduction for my children's college education? Two of my children will start college in a couple of years, and it's going to be tough to find the money to put them through school. Any recommendations?

A. Yes! The "income-splitting" devices covered in this chapter provide an indirect way of making your children's college costs tax-deductible. Here's how you do it:

Suppose you have a savings program for "children's college fund." (If you don't have one, you'd better start one quickly.) The money for college is in a money market fund yielding 12% annually. Unfortunately, you are a business executive in the 50% tax bracket, so that *half* of your money market fund earnings are going to the government.

After reading this chapter, you decide to solve this problem by granting an *interest-free loan to your children!* You lend them the funds in the money market fund, and they in turn place the funds in *another* money market fund under their own names. Your children are now earning 12% on money to be used for college, and therefore the income from the money funds is declared on *their* tax returns. The first $1,000 per child is completely free of income taxes, and earnings after that are taxed at a low 12% rate!

You are earning the same amount of interest income as before. But now you are paying little or nothing in taxes on the college account. The result is the same as if you had taken a tax deduction for the income made on the money fund. You have essentially taken a tax deduction for your children's college education!

4
—Tax-Free Fringe Benefits

A CHAUFFEURED limousine picks you up every morning, allowing you to read the paper or catch an extra snooze on the way to work . . . the dentist reports three cavities during your son's checkup, and you don't even think of the cost . . . you are covered by $50,000 worth of life insurance, but you've never paid a single premium . . . when a neighbor slips on a patch of ice and sues you for damages, your company lawyer defends you—*free* . . . you own twice as much stock in your company as you actually paid for . . . you spend your lunch hour working out at a posh athletic club without ever paying a membership fee, or sharing lunch with your child in the company-subsidized cafeteria . . . at night, you take your whole family to a baseball game using free company passes. . . .

Sounds like the kind of dream that is usually ended all too soon by the rude jangling of an alarm clock, doesn't it? But this dream has come true for many people employed by businesses that understand the value of offering fringe benefits instead of just higher salaries.

The financial advantages of fringe benefits are clear. Because of heavy taxation, nearly half of the average raise goes to the government, not to the employee. But since fringe benefits are not considered taxable income in most cases, an employee can receive an increase in compensation without increasing his tax liability.

THE COMMON SENSE OF FRINGE BENEFITS

Suppose you earn $30,000 a year, and you think it's time for a raise. Your employer agrees with you, but the question is, how much? If he gives you a straight 10% raise, your gross income increases by $3,000. His costs are actually a little more than that, because he must pay additional social security and unemployment premiums on your additional income. But let's look at your take-home pay. The marginal tax rate on your increase will be 33% or about $1,000. Another $200 goes to social security, and your state and local governments could require $300 or more. You are left with a little more than half of what your employer paid you.

But suppose you explore the possibilities of fringe benefits. Group insurance plans are a good example. If you bought an individual policy to cover major medical expenses, your annual premiums could cost as much as $1,500, equivalent to the after-tax yield on your raise. However, if your employer decides to purchase a group medical plan for all his employees, your net result is the same, but you have not moved into a higher tax bracket and your employer has saved additional employment taxes by not paying you a higher salary. That savings can be passed on to you in the form of additional fringe benefits, or to customers in the form of reduced prices for the company products. When Uncle Sam loses, everyone else gains!

Not surprisingly, the IRS has been fighting fringe benefits for years, insisting that they are taxable income. Fortunately, Congress has thwarted these efforts so far, recently imposing a moratorium on any IRS administrative rulings on fringe benefits until 1984.

Anyone who works can take advantage of fringe benefits. Whether you're a salaried employee, a company president or executive, or someone who is self-employed, you can enjoy the benefits of "perks." These benefits are deductible to the employer as a business expense, but they are free of income taxes to the employee. As long as tax rates remain high, the range of fringe benefits will continue to grow rapidly.

Let's examine some of the more popular areas of fringe benefits.

PENSION AND PROFIT-SHARING PLANS

Many companies offer valuable pension programs to their executives and employees of long standing. The retirement benefits alone can be outstanding, providing lifetime income that may even be greater than social security benefits, depending on the type of pension program your company sets up and the length of time you have been contributing to it.

But the tax benefits of a corporate pension plan can be very attractive as well. Your company can put as much as 15–25% of your salary into the retirement fund, and the amount will not be treated as taxable income until you retire and begin receiving benefits. This is actually a tax-*deferral* strategy, not a tax-*exempt* benefit. The theory is that since your income will most likely be much lower after you retire than it is while you are working, your tax bracket will also be lower, so you end up paying less to the government. Tax deferral always has another advantage, too, in the fact that you are able to invest that money and keep it working for you so that by the time you do owe the tax, you have more money than you started with. The wonders of tax-free compounding can astound you! Additionally, when you finally do pay the revenue man, you will almost certainly pay in greatly depreciated dollars.

By the same token, pension funds can be very expensive to the employer. This is why employees are often required to work for a certain number of years before they can qualify to participate in the company pension plan. Retirement benefits become an incentive for loyal employees to stay with the same company for a long time.

MEDICAL BENEFITS

One of the most common fringe benefits involves health benefits. These may include employer-paid medical insurance and reimbursement plans, employer-paid dental expenses, and long-term-disability insurance premiums.

At first glance, personal medical expenses appear to be tax-deductible. But there are severe limitations set by the IRS as to how much an individual can deduct. You may only deduct expenses that are greater than 5% of your income. Consequently, unless you are either very poor or very sick, medical expenses are not really tax-deductible. This is why employer-paid health benefits are so desirable.

Some companies offer to pay all medical premiums and expenses beyond a small deductible, typically the first $100 each year. Annual medical examinations, free to the employee, are sometimes included in this package.

Another sick-leave benefit provided by some companies is an end-of-the-year bonus equal to the amount of sick leave you did not use. This discourages employees from calling in sick when they are just sick of working, since in essence they receive double pay for days of unused sick leave.

If an employer provides long-term disability insurance, the premiums are tax-free, but if the employee should become disabled, the benefits are generally taxable as income. However, if the employee pays the premiums himself and then becomes disabled, the benefits would not be taxable income. Benefits are not limited to work-related accidents, and can involve permanent-disability insurance, death benefits to survivors, and a $5,000 tax-free payment to your heirs.

Finally, a relatively new addition to health benefits, dental insurance or employer-paid dental expenses is gaining rapid popularity at the bargaining table.

Medical premiums are also free from social security and unemployment taxes.

STOCK OWNERSHIP PLANS

Most major corporations offer matching savings plans to company employees, to encourage them to invest in the company. The company agrees to match employees' share purchases up to a certain limit. If an employee purchases 50 shares, the company may give him an additional 50 shares. The value of these shares is not taxed until the employee decides to sell, and even then they are taxed as long-term capital gains, which are 60% tax-free. Most companies have an upper limit on how much they will match, generally equal to 10–15% of the employee's earnings. Others match only a portion of the employee's savings, say 50¢ or 75¢ to the dollar rather than one to one.

Clearly, this is a lucrative way to save. In fact, some employees actually borrow money to invest with, just to take advantage of the full matching benefit. Unfortunately, however, a lot of blue-chip companies have seen their stocks fall in value during recent years, leaving participants with little real advantage. Invest in a company-matching plan only if the long-term outlook for the company is good.

NEW BALL GAME IN STOCK OPTIONS

Executives may take advantage of liberalized rules on stock options. Top company officials can receive options to purchase up to $100,000 in shares at below-market prices, and not be taxed on any gain until the shares are sold. The maximum tax rate on the long-term gain will be 20%. Certain qualifications must be met, but they are fairly easy. The executive must wait at least two years before exercising the option, and another year before selling the shares.

EMPLOYER-PAID MEALS

The IRS has been fighting a long battle against company-paid meals for employees. Under current rules, the value of a meal is not taxable income to the employee if it is furnished on business premises and is for the "convenience of the employer." It must also be a condition of employment.

EDUCATIONAL EXPENSES

An employer-paid educational program can be established for employees, and as long as it doesn't discriminate in favor of officers and executives, it is treated as tax-free income. Payments may include the cost of tuition, fees, and books, but not the cost of transportation. And, believe it or not, the courses need not be job-related!

FINANCIAL AND LEGAL COUNSELING

One of the most recent additions to the fringe-benefit package is group coverage of legal expenses, offered on a nondiscriminatory basis. With the incidence of legal action increasing throughout the United States, the chances that you will someday be involved in a court suit are high. Even if you win the suit, you could still be a loser because of the high cost of legal counsel. Company-paid "lawyer insurance" helps to defray that cost.

In addition, some companies now provide financial counseling, analyzing investment portfolios and showing employees how they can develop better savings habits and take advantage of the profit potential in stocks, bonds, mutual funds, and gold.

GIFTS AND AWARDS TO EMPLOYEES

Many company officers like to show their appreciation for valuable employees by giving them gifts or cash awards. Employers may deduct only $25 per gift per employee each year, but awards are far more flexible in monetary terms. As long as the employee has not entered a contest to receive the award, the company can deduct up to $1,600 for an award to an employee, and the award is not considered taxable income to the recipient either. An employee might be cited for his exemplary safety record, productivity, or length of service. Employee awards are a good way for companies to increase the monetary rewards of workers without increasing their tax liabilities.

DAY CARE

As more and more women enter the work force, finding reliable and reasonably priced day care has become a growing concern. The IRS allows a small child-care tax credit for parents who work. Some employers have gone a step further by providing day-care centers at the place of employment. The advantages are many: Commuting time is shortened, since both parent and child go to the same place; there are no early-morning calls from sick sitters unable to tend;

and the parent can spend lunch hour and coffee breaks with the child, if desired.

LIFE INSURANCE

Companies that provide group life insurance plans can give employees up to $50,000 worth of term insurance tax-free. Frequently, the actual amount of coverage will be equal to double the employee's salary, or will be linked to some other standard measurement.

Employers can also provide life insurance beyond the $50,000 level, but the additional premiums are taxable to individual employees as income, according to IRS standards. A new fringe benefit has been the creation of "retired life reserves," a program that pays term insurance premiums for employees after they retire. The company creates a "reserve fund" whose purpose is to pay the premiums in the future. Contributions to the fund are tax-deductible to the corporation, and the earnings from the fund accumulate tax-free. An insurance company normally manages the reserve fund, but a company can set up its own trust to manage the money if it wishes. Employees never pay taxes on the fringe benefit, except that the premiums in excess of $50,000 worth of coverage are treated as taxable income. This kind of insurance program has not been particularly popular because of its inherent high cost (contributions are based on the cost of insurance at retirement age, which can be exorbitant). But for a small closely held corporation, it can be an ideal tax shelter.

OTHER EMPLOYEE BENEFITS

The list of fringe benefits is almost endless. Many companies are expanding the traditional benefits to include such areas as discounts on company items through a PX, company-subsidized cafeterias, low-interest or no-interest loans through company credit unions, and even turkeys, hams, and similar holiday items.

EXECUTIVE "PERKS"

There are many additional "executive perks" available to the top management in many corporations. I've already mentioned incentive stock options. Other tax-free benefits may include:

— a company car, possibly chauffeured, even for personal use
— residential security systems
— free reserved parking space
— free theater and sports tickets
— athletic club memberships
— use of corporate jet, resort area, or other luxuries

A recent study by the American Management Association discovered that of 731 major corporations surveyed, 68% supplied company cars (including personal use), 67% provided free medical exams, 61% had free reserved parking, 56% gave away athletic-club memberships, 33% offered personal-finance planning, 25% distributed free theater and sports tickets, and 16% provided legal counseling. Personal use of corporate jets, executive hunting lodges, vacation resorts, and luxury yacht cruises were on the decline, however. The Revenue Act of 1978 did much to limit these kinds of company-paid activities.

Fringe-benefit programs are not supposed to discriminate in favor of executives, but they are often more advantageous to the highly paid worker. For example, life insurance coverage and pension contributions may be tied to the employee's salary. As a result, higher-paid employees will receive greater benefits.

FRINGE BENEFITS FOR THE SELF-EMPLOYED

A part-time business, a one-man company, or a closely held corporation can still take advantage of many fringe-benefit programs. The owner of a single proprietorship could establish a Keogh plan for himself and his employees, as well as health, educational, or other benefits. A corporation offers an even wider selection. The corporate pension plan is far more flexible and permits greater contributions than a Keogh plan. You can put up to 25% of most employees' salaries into a corporate pension plan, and even more for older employees under a "defined benefit" plan. A corporation can also offer an incentive stock-option plan for top management, and company-matching programs. A corporate structure clearly offers the widest variety of fringe-benefit opportunities.

FRINGE BENEFITS FOR MILITARY PERSONNEL AND VETERANS

A chapter on fringe benefits would not be complete without mentioning the incredible benefits offered to members of the armed forces and their families. It is estimated that fringe benefits can amount to 75% of salary compensation in the military! These tax-free benefits include full medical and dental care, life insurance, travel expenses, PX privileges, GI educational payments, housing allowances, and combat pay. In addition, military personnel may select a home state for tax purposes, rather than claiming the state where they are currently living. This can mean significant savings for someone stationed in Massachusetts or New York, for example.

HOW TO BENEFIT

Investigate the tremendous variety of fringe benefits available in your company—in many cases, they can amount to 25–30% of your overall compensation. Don't think just in terms of a cash salary when applying for a raise. Make sure your company is aware of the many fringe benefits it can offer.

But remember that while fringe benefits may be *tax*-free, they are not *cost*-free to the business. It's true that they are *deductible* as business expenses, but the *after-tax* expense of fringe benefits can still be sizable. Consequently, companies can only expand their fringe benefits as they grow in size and profit margins.

Problem Solver #3

Q. I'm thinking of asking for a raise where I work, but when I found out that 44% of the raise would go toward federal and state income taxes, not to mention higher social security, I decided I might as well forget it. Is there any way around this problem?

A. There are a number of ways you can get a raise without having to pay more in taxes. Make your company aware of the wide variety of valuable fringe benefits it can offer to employees in lieu of direct increases in income. It's an educational process, but when the employer sees that the fringe benefits are tax-deductible to the company and tax-free to the employee, the employer should realize immediately that *everyone* is better off when fringe benefits are substituted for pay raises. In fact, the employer can save money all around, because most employees would prefer to have a valuable fringe benefit tax-free rather than a pay raise that means a higher tax bracket. Some overlooked fringe benefits include an awards program, medical care paid entirely by the company, financial counseling, and educational expenses. Such expenditures can be extremely valuable to employees, and much appreciated.

5
━━ Living Abroad
Tax-Free

NEXT JANUARY, while your neighbors are chipping the ice off their sidewalks, you could invite them to come visit you at your villa in Mexico City, your beach house in the Bahamas, or your condominium on the French Riviera ... in early summer, when tourists begin to cover the beaches, you could move to your chalet on the outskirts of Zurich or to your flat in London ... all of Europe tends to close up in August, so you fly back to the States for three weeks of fresh peaches and corn on the cob ... Spain is beautiful in the fall, particularly near the Pyrenees, so you spend the rest of the year in southern Europe ... but Christmas wouldn't be Christmas without the extended family, so you jet back home to Minnesota for two weeks of family reunions, snow, and Viking football games.

But perhaps you don't like that much traveling. You're a home-body; you like to set down roots. In that case, you might prefer a more permanent domicile in a cosmopolitan center such as Paris, London, or Hong Kong. Or, if peace and quiet are what you crave, try a quiet little village in Costa Rica, Argentina, or the Cayman Islands.

No matter what country you finally choose, the tax advantages may be outstanding: Americans living abroad can now earn up to $75,000 *each*, completely free of onerous U.S. taxation. If both husband and wife are employed overseas, they could earn as much as $150,000 and keep every cent. The exemption increases each year until, by 1986, each American can earn up to $95,000 tax-free, simply by living and working outside the country. For someone in the 50% tax bracket, this represents an overwhelming tax savings.

What has brought about this change?

For decades the tax burden for Americans living abroad was unbearable, and getting worse. Americans were required to pay taxes to the foreign governments where they lived and worked, while the U.S. government compounded the burden by imposing a complex set of special rules, exemptions, credits, and housing deductions. These usually resulted in *double taxation* of Americans living abroad. Needless to say, making your home in a foreign land was complicated, expensive, and frustrating.

But Reagan's Economic Recovery Act of 1981 has made a dramatic change in the tax laws governing nonresident citizens. It grants the overseas U.S. taxpayer the most important tax advantages ever, virtually eliminating the burden of double taxation for 90% of the Americans working in foreign lands. Because of these outstanding tax breaks, living outside the United States is no longer a luxury available only to the wealthy or the military. Living in a foreign country can be extremely attractive, especially in certain countries in Europe, Latin America, the Caribbean, and the Far East.

UP TO $75,000 AND MORE IN NEW TAX BREAKS

What exactly are these new tax advantages?

To begin with, expatriates (referring to U.S. citizens working abroad) can exclude up to $75,000 of *earned* income in 1982. This exclusion increases by $5,000 each year until 1986, when it reaches $95,000.

Foreign-based income is any income earned for services rendered outside the country. Your wages, salary, or commissions can come from a foreign company, a foreign government, or a U.S. company stationed abroad. It can even come from a domestic U.S. company, as long as you performed the service outside the country.

The new tax law (Section 911 of the U.S. Tax Code) allows the tax exclusion on earned income only, not investment or so-called "unearned" income.

Second, an additional tax break is given for *housing costs*. The exclusion is for housing expenses in excess of a base amount, which will increase each year according to federal pay raises. The current base amount is $6,350. Utilities and insurance qualify as housing expenses, but not interest and taxes, which are deductible separately.

In essence, expatriates will be able to write off their total housing costs if they itemize. Anyone who has lived overseas knows how expensive foreign living can be—annual housing expenses can exceed $50,000 a year for executives. Thus, adding the housing-cost exclusion to the earned-income exclusion, the tax break could exceed $100,000 per person or $175,000 for a two-income family.

Third, expatriates are charged lower tax rates on interest, dividends, annuities, and other *investment income*. This "unearned" income is taxed at the same marginal tax rates as for all U.S. taxpayers, but because of the earned-income exclusion of $75,000 or more, the tax rates on *unearned* income will begin at 12% (the lowest tax bracket). By contrast, stateside taxpayers pay the *highest* marginal tax rate on their investment income, as much as 50%.

Fourth, *U.S. social security or self-employment taxes* can be avoided. A U.S. citizen employed by a U.S. employer is subject to the social security tax even when working in a foreign country. A foreign corporation owned wholly or in part by a U.S. corporation may choose to arrange with the IRS to provide FICA coverage to its employees, but it is not required to do so. But U.S. employees of *foreign* corporations are not subject to the FICA tax because the foreign country usually has its own form of social security. Of course, this can be an advantage or a disadvantage, depending on the country in which you reside. At any rate, if you do pay into a foreign social program, you will qualify for foreign benefits.

Self-employed expatriates who are bona fide residents of a foreign country can avoid the social security tax altogether as long as their earned income does not exceed the $75,000 (or more) exclusions and deductions.

HOW TO QUALIFY

The new law makes it easier for U.S. taxpayers to qualify for the foreign income tax exclusion. You need to fulfill the requirements of one of two tests:

1. *Physical presence test.* This test has become much easier to fulfill than it was in the past. To qualify, you do not have to establish an official residence in a foreign country, but you do have to remain outside the United States at least 330 days in a 12-month period.

This leaves you with the opportunity of spending 35 days, or 5 weeks, within the United States each year. Under this arrangement, you do not have to remain in a single foreign country for the entire 330 days, but you do need to maintain an address in a foreign country as your "tax home." Otherwise, you will simply be considered an American on an extended vacation and will not qualify for the income exclusion.

2. *Bona fide residence test.* To qualify for this test, you should file for "permanent residence" with a foreign government, and live there for an entire taxable year. Once you have established residence, you can amend your older tax return to claim the exclusion for any portion of the year that you were outside the U.S. After you establish foreign residency, you are allowed to travel in the United States much more frequently than under the physical presence test. In fact, there is technically no limitation on how often you can travel in the States as long as you remain a "permanent resident" of another country! The accounting firm Price Waterhouse warns, however, that "remaining in the United States for, say, nine months will almost always mean that the abode is in the United States. . . . it would be prudent for an otherwise qualified individual to avoid remaining in the United States for extended periods of time."

Once you become a foreign resident, U.S. taxation may not be your only concern. You must now worry about *foreign* income taxes. The rates in some countries are even higher than in the U.S., while other countries' taxes are all but nonexistent. In addition, some countries require you to live in a country for at least six months to be a "permanent resident," a restriction you may not like.

NEW OPPORTUNITIES IN OVERSEAS EMPLOYMENT

It may seem that now all you have to do is decide where in all the world you want to live, but there is still one other important factor to consider before you can take advantage of this new tax exclusion. That is, how are you going to earn as much as $75,000 while living abroad?

A self-employed American, particularly in such free-lance areas as consulting, writing, research, photography, and acting, might find it relatively easy to set up shop in another country. But those whose skills demand working for someone else have several opportunities available to them as well.

Is it possible that the company you presently work for could profit from a representative in a foreign country? What special skills do you possess that would make you the right person for an overseas assignment? Once you have prepared a strong case, present it to your company for approval.

If your company isn't interested in sending you abroad, begin exploring outside alternatives. A large number of corporations need qualified personnel to represent them abroad, but quite often they are unable to find current employees willing to go. These corporations strongly lobbied for the new tax law in an effort to alleviate the overseas tax burden for their U.S. employees. Now that the law has passed, major corporations will undoubtedly be seeking new talent for overseas assignments.

There are many U.S.-based hotel chains, airlines, oil companies, accounting firms, financial institutions, publishing companies, recording firms, and other major corporations with offices and services throughout the world. Often these companies turn to executive search organizations or employment agencies to help them find suitable personnel. Contact the corporations yourself, or send résumés to top-notch executive-search firms, outlining your interest in working abroad. They will interview you when the right job comes along.

You might also consider getting involved in a foreign franchise of an American company. McDonald's restaurants and Pizza Huts are springing up all over the world, and the popularity of American-style food is growing rapidly. During a recent trip to London, we noticed that locally run pubs and cafés had empty tables, while the lines at McDonald's were long. In fact, when we passed by at lunchtime one day the lines were clear out the door to the sidewalk! Clearly, the foreign demand for American fast food is greater than the supply.

Finally, consider employment with a foreign firm. Each country has its own rules governing work permits and residency requirements, so you will have to do your own investigating to find, and then qualify for, foreign employment.

MOVING TO A FOREIGN LAND

If you decide to move out of the United States, you can deduct the cost of travel for yourself and your family, including the cost of shipping your household goods. You can also deduct the cost of a pre-moving house-hunting trip and temporary living costs up to $4,500. You can even deduct the cost of storing goods while you are abroad. If your moving expenses are reimbursed by your company, they are treated as earned income—but they qualify for the Section 911 tax-free exclusion.

What about your current residence in the States? Normally, when you sell your home, you must repurchase another home within two years in order to defer taxes on the capital gains. But if you sell your home and move abroad, you have *four years* to buy another principal residence before you would lose the tax deferral on the gain on the home. Thus, you could sell your home and rent overseas for up to four years before deciding whether to buy again.

Another possibility is to retain your U.S. home and rent it while you're away. This is a popular alternative that does not jeopardize your status as a nonresident. Rental income is reportable, but with most real estate today, the deductions for interest, taxes, and depreciation tend to balance the income. When you return to the States, you can again live in your home without any current tax liability.

U.S. TAX OBLIGATIONS

While the investment returns of a U.S. citizen living abroad may be free of taxes in the adopted country, the U.S. tax on "unearned" (investment) income is another story. As stated in the beginning of this chapter, the U.S. tax exclusion for U.S. citizens working abroad applies only to *earned* income. Investment income is taxed as it is in the States, at rates up to 50%, depending on the amount. The only legal way to completely avoid all U.S. income tax is to become a permanent citizen of another country and renounce your U.S. citizenship. Even then, if the IRS can show that you renounced your citizenship to reduce or eliminate your U.S. tax obligations, it may continue to tax you for another 10 years! There are ways around this arbitrary IRS action, but they are complex and require the help of a tax specialist.

Here's an alternative that may be advantageous to retirees living in a foreign country: Place all your investments in a foreign investment company, and then have the company pay you a salary for managing the company's investments. In essence you have changed your "unearned" income, which is taxable, into "earned" income, which is tax-free up to the foreign-income exclusion. The IRS might challenge this method, but you have a good case if you are an aggressive trader, switching investments frequently for maximum return. After all, the IRS itself argues that an investor who trades too frequently is engaged in a trade or business, and therefore has "earned" income. Check with your tax adviser before trying this approach; there may be hidden drawbacks, such as earning too much to qualify for social security benefits if you are over 65.

WHAT ABOUT STATE INCOME TAXES?

Even though you live abroad, some states may argue that you are still a local resident and therefore must pay income taxes. These states figure that you're still a state resident unless you can demonstrate that you do not intend to return. Bizarre as it may seem, some states will go to great lengths to tax you. If, for example, you maintain ownership of a home while you are away, the state may use this as proof that you are a resident, and will place a lien against the property if you do not pay the tax willingly. This makes as much sense as saying that a person must be taxed as a resident of five states, just because he owns rental property in five states. If you live in such a state, the best way to solve the problem is to establish official residency status in a foreign country, and to sever all economic relationships with the state, including property ownership.

WHICH COUNTRIES ARE BEST?

In choosing a place to live, tax avoidance isn't the only consideration, nor should it even be your primary consideration. Other important concerns include climate, language, culture, cost of living, communications facilities, job opportunities, social amenities, and ease of travel. More important, the new U.S. tax law only reduces the taxes on one side of the "double taxation" equation. Each country has its own set of complex tax, work, and residency requirements, which you must evaluate according to your personal situation. This chapter is only intended to get you started—you should do a good deal of personal research before making a decision.

Your first choice for living abroad might be major Western countries such as Canada, Germany, or France. Canada, for instance, is right next door, and is culturally similar to the States. English is spoken, business is favorable, sports and other activities are similar, and the democratic government allows a great deal of personal freedom.

Unfortunately, Canada and most other major nations are not a tax haven for Americans working abroad. They impose taxes that are just as stiff as those in the States, and foreigners are not exempt if they become residents.

Britain: The New U.S. Tax Haven

Great Britain, however, may be an exciting exception to this rule. Several years ago, the British government created a tax holiday for foreigners. This law, which will be in effect until 1990, allows foreigners who work for foreign-based companies to declare only 50% of their income on British tax returns. This represents a substantial savings, but since British taxes are very high, the *maximum* income rate would still be about 41%, a sizable burden.

However, the British have provided an advantage that is even more important. Foreigners working for a third country, and being paid in a third country, do not have to pay British taxes, even while residing in Britain. Thus, if you have your income credited to a bank account in a third country (such as Switzerland) and use investments and other funds for living expenses while in Britain, you achieve a considerable tax savings! This so-called split-contract system is well established by foreign firms in Britain, and is recognized and accepted by the British Inland Revenue. Japan, Belgium, and other countries have similar arrangements for split-contract workers.

The British Isles may be a first choice for many Americans because of the cultural, social, and financial advantages. London is an international financial center, with full-service banking, worldwide brokerage services, and ready markets in commodities, metals, stocks, bonds, and collectibles. Many U.S. companies use London as a base for European operations because of the common language. The night life is great, with first-rate plays, musicals, and movies—a cultural mecca. Although England is not known for its culinary talent, there are nevertheless many good ethnic restaurants in the cities.

A sense of history permeates all of London; the worlds of Dickens and Henry VIII live side by side with massive bank buildings and modern clothing stores. And just minutes outside the bustling cosmopolitan center of London, pastoral England awaits. This truly is a country that has something for everyone.

There are excellent communications and flight connections from England to the Continent and the rest of the world, making this a convenient home-away-from-home for Americans living abroad.

Monaco

Monaco, an independent principality since 1511, is a city comprising just one half square mile, sandwiched between Southern France and Italy. The city itself, called Monte Carlo, is a delightful cosmopolitan resort, known for its night life, gambling, warm climate, and wealthy citizens. Many Europeans come to Monte Carlo and the Riviera to vacation.

Amazingly, 85% of Monaco's inhabitants are expatriates! Besides the ambience, the main attraction is a low tax rate. Monaco has neither property tax nor capital gains tax. Foreigners pay no income taxes at all, although there is a 35% corporate tax for foreign-based businesses. Establishing residency is fairly easy for an American, if you can afford the sky-high real estate and cost of living there.

Caribbean and Latin America

To many Americans, the real "American dream" means leaving the fast-paced, highly competitive urban life behind them in favor of the easygoing life of an island paradise. An early-morning swim in the warm surf, breakfast of freshly picked fruits and rich Jamaican coffee, an afternoon of sailing or just napping in the salty breeze, and a moonlight stroll under a million stars may seem the ideal life, particularly for those who have worked long hard hours to become successful and now want to enjoy some of the fruits of their labor.

The Bahamas, the Cayman Islands, and other small countries in the Caribbean have many attributes that make them attractive for offshore living and working.

The Commonwealth of the Bahamas is probably the most famous tax haven known to Americans. There are no income taxes, no estate taxes, and no gift taxes. The local government pays its way largely through import duties and corporate licensing fees. Nassau, the capital, is a large financial center, with branches of major U.S., Canadian, and Swiss banks established there. The commonwealth also has a well-established bank secrecy law, and has no tax treaty with any country.

The Bahamas enjoy balmy, warm climate year-round, as well as clean air and beautiful water. The islands are only 75 miles off the Florida coast, so travel and communications are excellent, with direct-dial telephone to the United States. Thousands of tourists visit Freeport, Nassau, and the out islands every year.

Setting up residency in the Bahamas is much more difficult than in other nations around the world. Just applying for permanent residence costs $5,000. The applicant cannot engage in a business without a "work permit," and if he applies for a work permit, he must show that a Bahamian is not available for the job. If he does not get a work permit, he must prove to the Bahamian government that he can live without working. In the end, most of the foreigners who have obtained bona fide residency in the Bahamas are extremely wealthy, obtaining their income from outside sources, or are engaged in creative freelance work. Arthur Hailey and other authors have found the quiet pace of the Bahamas to be particularly conducive to productive writing.

If you cannot get a work permit and do not want to reveal your financial status to the Bahamian government, there is another alternative. Tourists may stay in the Bahamas for up to six months without a visa. Therefore, you could simply stay in the Bahamas for six months, leave for a few days or weeks, and then return. You would thus fulfill the U.S. physical presence test by remaining outside the U.S. for 330 days, thereby qualifying for the income tax exclusion in the United States. Make sure, however, that you do not engage in any income-producing business inside the Bahamas—all your earnings should come from the United States or other countries.

Investing in Bahamian real estate has been popular over the years, especially in Nassau and Freeport. There has been some concern over efforts by the Bahamian government to restrict land sales, but well-established real estate should still be marketable. There should be no problem if you buy property for a personal residence, or you can always rent a place instead.

The political situation in the Bahamas has been relatively stable since blacks achieved independence on the islands in 1973.

The Cayman Islands are located south of Cuba and west of Jamaica, about 475 miles from Miami. A self-governing British colony, Cayman is stable politically and booming economically.

Like the Bahamas, Cayman has no direct form of taxation, is not party to any tax treaties, and has strict bank secrecy laws. Branches of major banks and insurance companies are located on Grand Cayman Island. Real estate is booming on Grand Cayman, and is definitely worth investigating as an investment for Americans. There are no restrictions on foreign ownership of Cayman properties or condominiums. Amazingly, there are no property taxes in Cayman!

Living in the Caymans as an expatriate is not difficult. A residency permit is required, but is easily obtained, particularly if your work is in a specialized field or involves income from abroad. The amenities and cultural activities are sparse in this little Caribbean island, however—buying videocassette tapes of Miami TV shows is very popular!

Cayman is growing so fast that communications facilities have increased tremendously in the past few years. Direct-dial telephoning is now available to most parts of the U.S., Canada, and Great Britain. Direct flights come from Miami and Houston.

Like the Bahamas and Bermuda, Cayman is known for its banking facilities, and the establishment of corporations, trusts, and insurance companies. Cayman has recently established itself as a premier international tax haven.

Costa Rica has been of considerable interest to Americans as a tax haven. Costa Rica does not tax foreigners on their foreign-based income. It also has tight secrecy laws, and is not a party to any tax treaties with other countries. Income earned from Costa Rican sources would be taxable, but most Americans would not have this problem. Thus, Costa Rica may be an ideal tax haven for the American earning his income from the United States and abroad.

Costa Rica has been a popular place for Americans to retire.

Currently about 15,000 Americans live in or near the capital city of San José, enjoying the year-round springlike weather, the friendly people, and the low prices.

Americans can become residents of Costa Rica through compliance with its very liberal 1971 Retirement Law, which provides residency and a provisional passport to foreigners. In order to qualify, an American must demonstrate proof that he has at least $300 in monthly income. This money can come from social security or a private pension (making one a "resident pensioner" or *pensionado*) or from investments from outside Costa Rica (making one a "resident investor"). One can even purchase a certificate of deposit from a Costa Rican bank with a return sufficient to meet the $300-a-month requirement. None of the interest or dividends is taxed by the Costa Rican government.

In addition, the applicant must provide a police certificate stating that he does not have a criminal record, and that he is not involved in any illegal activities.

Finally, to receive a Costa Rican passport, an applicant is required to produce his current passport, a marriage certificate if the spouse is to be included as a dependent, and birth certificates of any dependent children. Also, the applicant will need to maintain at least $10,000 in Costa Rican real estate for as long as he owns a Costa Rican passport.

Warning: Obtaining a Costa Rican passport may jeopardize your U.S. citizenship, so consult with your attorney before taking this important step.

To obtain residency status, you are supposed to live in Costa Rica at least six months out of the year. In the past, many Americans have not complied with this requirement, and, by putting up additional funds, have been exempt from the six-month rule. However, because of increasing abuse, Costa Rica has recently rescinded the issuance of passports on this basis.

The provisional or temporary passport is good for five years, after which a permanent passport will be issued. The Costa Rican passport, whether provisional or permanent, is accepted by virtually all nations, and you should have no problem traveling on this passport.

Americans are still welcomed by the Costa Rican people. There are very few restrictions placed on foreigners by the Costa Rican government. There is, on the other hand, legitimate concern over the long-term stability of a nation so closely situated between Panama and Nicaragua. Costa Rica's communist party is not large, but the country has no standing army to protect its borders from foreign invaders. In addition, the Costa Rican economy is in serious trouble. Inflation is raging at 40% a year, and Costa Rica has stopped paying off its international debt. Whoever said Costa Rica was the "Switzerland of the Americas" must surely have changed his mind by now.

Hong Kong

Lying around the beach sipping piña coladas for more than a week-long vacation might drive some people crazy, no matter what the tax advantages. If you thrive on noise, people, and constant activity, then perhaps Hong Kong is the place for you.

As an independent British colony, Hong Kong combines aspects of several cultures to make it an Asian country that is uniquely Western. Unexcelled oriental craftsmanship combines with free-market principles to provide the best shopping in the world for textiles, ceramics, and handcrafted items. Ethnic restaurants offer every style of food, from French to Indian to, of course, Chinese. American TV shows are available on several channels, with one delightful omission—there are hardly any commercials! A major advantage for U.S. expatriates is that English is the official language.

Hong Kong charges a low tax rate of 17% on all domestic income, but it imposes no income tax at all on *foreign-based* income. There is no Hong Kong tax on capital gains or dividends, although interest from local bank accounts is assessed. Hong Kong has no tax treaty with other countries.

As the financial center of Southeast Asia, Hong Kong has good business connections with China, Australia, and Singapore. It is a leading manufacturing and trading center, targeting the United States as a major market. It is connected by major airlines with all parts of the world, and has excellent communications by telex or telephone.

Americans living and working in Hong Kong have many advantages. English is used for most business transactions. Bank and brokerage facilities are excellent. There are virtually no restrictions on U.S. citizens living and working in Hong Kong, although the British colony is attempting to limit Chinese refugees. Expatriates from other nations also view Hong Kong as a tax and political refuge, resulting in a multinational atmosphere in the tiny British colony.

Other Countries

There are still other countries that could qualify as tax havens for Americans. For example, in Latin America, the countries of Argentina, Uruguay, Venezuela, and Panama have tax advantages similar to those in Costa Rica. If you prefer the Far East, Taiwan and Japan have some interesting advantages. Self-employed entrepreneurs with Taiwan-based businesses are practically exempt from Taiwanese income taxes. In addition, Taiwan does not tax foreign-based income at all. Japan, like Britain, permits split contracts so that earnings paid to a third country are exempt from Japanese taxes.

SIX-MONTH LOOPHOLE?

There is one other alternative that we have not explored regarding tax-free living abroad. You may still prefer to live in Germany, France, or another major nation that imposes high taxes on a foreigner's income. As a general rule, most major countries tax the worldwide income of all residents. But they usually define a "resident" as one who lives in the country at least six months during the year. Therefore, if you stay in any one country for only six months, you can completely avoid foreign income taxes, while still qualifying for the U.S. income tax exclusion through the physical presence test. You could have a summer home in Europe and a winter resort in the Caribbean or Mexico, and travel within the states for up to five weeks. As Doug Casey writes in *The International Man*, "It's quite possible to pay no tax at all legally. This is often what some of the world's richest people do." By using this method, you can consider living in practically any country in the world—Germany, France, England, Mexico, Japan, etc.

But you do have to be careful with U.S. tax authorities. Taking an inconsistent position on your foreign residence, or "tax home," can jeopardize your eligibility for the Section 911 exclusion. For example, if an expatriate submits a statement to officials of a foreign country claiming to be a nonresident to avoid that country's taxes, he could not qualify as a bona fide resident of that country under Section 911 for the U.S. tax exclusion. He must then use the physical presence test of 330 days abroad in 12 months. The burden of proof for using this test falls on the taxpayer. Strict travel records should be maintained.

If an expatriate does not become a full-time resident of another country, he must nevertheless establish a "tax home," or he will lose the foreign-earned income provisions. "Tax home" would typically refer to the location where the taxpayer earns most of his income, or where his trade or business is conducted. But as Peat, Marwick, Mitchell & Co. point out, "The new shortened time periods in the physical presence test . . . may raise tax home questions, especially in situations where the taxpayer also maintains a residence in the U.S. Thus, taxpayers relying on the physical presence test should carefully document that a foreign country is their tax home."

IS EMIGRATION FOR YOU?

It's a sad commentary on today's world that taxation has become a prime consideration in deciding where to live. If all governments followed Hong Kong's example of limited government and a low, flat tax rate, we could concentrate on earning more, rather than worrying about how to keep what we've already earned. But when deciding whether emigration is for you, remember that social, cultural, and patriotic interests may be far more important than financial goals. If you can combine an all-round personal satisfaction with low-tax living by moving to a foreign country, you will be that much better off.

RECOMMENDED READING

The big eight account firms (Price Waterhouse; Peat, Marwick, Mitchell; Coopers & Lybrand; Ernst & Whinney; etc.) publish pamphlets which detail the dramatic changes in the tax law as they affect U.S. workers abroad. They have offices throughout the country and abroad. Ask for their publications on tax planning for overseas taxpayers. Three recommended publications are:

"Impact of the new 1981 U.S. Tax Law on Americans Abroad," published by Price Waterhouse, 1251 Ave. of the Americas, New York, NY 10020.
"U.S. Expatriate Taxation," published by Peat, Marwick, Mitchell & Co., 345 Park Ave., New York, NY 10022.
"Expatriate Tax Planning," published by Coopers & Lybrand, 1251 Ave. of the Americas, New York, NY 10020.

I also recommend *The International Man,* by Douglas R. Casey (Alexandria House Books, 1300 N. 17th St., Arlington, VA 22209; 1981 edition, $14.95).

Problem Solver #4

Q. I'm a freelance writer. Last year I paid $10,000 in federal and state income taxes and nearly $3,000 in self-employment tax. Do you have any recommendations for reducing my tax burden?

A. You could take advantage of some tax shelters here in the United States, but a better idea might be to move outside the United States for a few years and take advantage of the $75,000 foreign income exclusion. Several countries offer tax breaks for U.S. citizens living abroad. Ireland provides a liberal tax-free opportunity for artists and writers who reside there. Some Caribbean or Latin American countries, such as Costa Rica, have no income tax at all for foreigners. If you become a resident, you can avoid the self-employment tax. Since you are a freelance writer, you could probably live in one of several countries tax-free and still avoid U.S. taxes by qualifying under the physical presence test. You could visit in the U.S. up to five weeks under this arrangement. Saving $10,000 might be worth it!

6

—The Advantages of Tax Havens

DON J. was flying back from a very successful trip in the Cayman Islands, a tiny dot in the Caribbean that is fast becoming a major international tax haven. An American businessman, Don decided several years ago to "go offshore" to avoid skyrocketing U.S. taxes. Several years before, on a business trip to London, he had met Stewart C., a like-minded British entrepreneur. They joined forces and formed a foreign corporation in the Caymans, each putting up equal capital and each owning half of the company shares. Because of this 50-50 partnership, the corporation legally avoided both U.S. and British taxation. Through the corporation, they could invest in virtually any investment vehicle. Recently, they purchased some fine paintings through a Christie's auction in London, and invested in some prime real estate in Monte Carlo. The corporation owns shares in a Eurocurrency fund, and dabbles in commodity futures in Chicago. Last year, the corporation earned over $100,000 in dividends and $50,000 in capital gains—completely tax-free. Both Don and Stewart spend time traveling to exotic places around the world, supervising their investments, all of which is a legitimate business expense. The corporation recently purchased a beachfront condo in the U.S. Virgin Islands, which they use personally when they get a chance and rent out for additional corporate income when they are away. If the corporation declared any dividends, Don would be liable for U.S. taxes, but Don is not interested in taking dividends, or in selling for that matter. He is content to let the money compound, tax-free, until he needs it for various uses. Perhaps his children can take advantage of the foreign corporation when they become of age, thus postponing his personal tax liability indefinitely. . . .

Even if you are not interested in living abroad, you may find it extremely valuable to set up a foreign trust or corporation that can be directed from within the United States. As Don J. learned, there are some unique tax savings and financial opportunities possible through the use of tax-haven facilities.

This chapter will examine the kinds of facilities available in Bermuda, the Caribbean, Europe, and other tax havens. Some of these facilities are completely legitimate for U.S. investors, and are sanctioned by the U.S. Tax Code. Others are shady, requiring the use of complex ways to bend the law. If the IRS discovers a shady deal and challenges it, you could be faced with additional taxes, interest, penalties, and even a jail sentence. Knowing the difference between legitimate and illegitimate tax-haven use is *vital*.

The U.S. Tax Code is very restrictive in what it legally allows you to do in offshore trusts or companies. There are a great many questionable schemes being established in the tax-haven countries in an unending frenzy to beat the taxman, but we will limit our recommendations to legitimate operations that stay within the U.S. law and that require the assistance of reputable legal counsel.

It is still possible, within certain limitations, to take advantage of tax-haven entities and legally postpone or eliminate U.S. tax liabilities. But you must be extremely careful in arranging your offshore affairs properly, not falling into the trap of relying solely on the secrecy laws of small islands in the sea.

IS A SECRET FOREIGN TRUST FOR YOU?

One arrangement of questionable legitimacy is the establishment of an "anonymous foreign trust" or a "bearer corporation" in countries that have strict secrecy. The big question is, are these secret entities legal or illegal for U.S. investors? How would the IRS treat these trusts and bearer corporations if it found out about them? Would users be subject to any civil or criminal penalties, or would they just owe back taxes plus interest, as some promoters have suggested?

U.S. tax law is the major deterrent to tax-haven use. There are many sections of the U.S. Tax Code that restrict or eliminate the tax advantages of foreign entities. The Tax Reform Act of 1976, in particular, closed a number of loopholes. Basically, the law now states that if a U.S. resident establishes a foreign trust (making him the "grantor"), administers the trust (making him the "trustee"), or is the ultimate recipient of the trust's funds (making him the "beneficiary"), he is required to pay taxes on any interest, dividends, or capital gains made by the trust. Prior to the 1976 Tax Reform Act, U.S. investors could establish an offshore trust and avoid taxes on profits until the money was actually "repatriated," or returned to the U.S. resident. But because the foreign trust had become a popular way to escape taxation or postpone it indefinitely, Congress changed the law.

Congress's change in the tax-haven legislation was aimed at completely eliminating this offshore loophole. But the international tax-haven community didn't give up easily. Many tax-haven attorneys came up with new ways to sidestep the U.S. regulations, at least on paper.

I recently visited the three most popular tax havens close to the United States: Bermuda, the Bahamas, and the Cayman Islands. There are a number of other tax havens, but I particularly focused on these three countries because of their proximity to the U.S. and because their tax-haven facilities are well established. Other tax-haven countries usually offer similar tax-saving plans.

Bermuda

Bermuda is regarded as a "first-class" tax haven. Located about 775 miles southeast of New York City, the island is a self-governing British colony. The country is still run largely by the white minority, which has caused occasional rioting by the blacks, who represent 60% of the population. When I visited Bermuda, I didn't sense any racial strife, but many predict a black-majority takeover in the near future. I doubt that this will have any negative effect on the financial community there, however.

As a tax haven, Bermuda has no tax on personal income, corporate income, or capital gains. It has no gift or estate taxes. It has no withholding tax, and no tax treaty with any country. It does not have an official secrecy law, but it has a strong tradition of confidentiality in its financial affairs. The island has only three banks, all Bermudian, and does not permit branches of foreign banks.

Some U.S. investors use Bermuda to establish an "anonymous trust," in an effort to avoid U.S. taxation. The foreign trust is set up by a Bermuda attorney, not by the U.S. resident, so the U.S. citizen is not officially the "grantor" of the trust. Second, the trustee is a Bermuda bank officer, so, at least on paper, the U.S. resident is not the "trustee." Third, the beneficiary is another person or perhaps a charitable organization. The beneficiaries could be the children of this "anonymous" U.S. citizen. Of course, they would be liable for the tax, even if they are unaware of the trust's existence, but presumably the children would be in a lower tax bracket. Thus, the U.S. investor is not the "beneficiary" of the trust, either.

This arrangement raises a lot of questions. If the U.S. resident gives up the right to be the grantor, the trustee, or the beneficiary, hasn't he lost control of his hard-earned money? Couldn't the trustee simply ignore the U.S. resident's investment instructions and invest any way the bank manager wished?

"Certainly," replied a Bermudian bank officer. "But I wouldn't do that because word would get around and I would lose the confidence of other clients coming to Bermuda to set up foreign trusts." The bank officer explained that he follows the instructions he receives from the U.S. citizen to the letter, investing in stocks, bonds, gold shares, precious metals, foreign currencies, diamonds, or whatever those instructions suggest.

Getting the money to Bermuda is another tricky maneuver. Unless the money came from "ill-gotten gains," there will be a record of the transfer to the foreign trust. If more than $10,000 a year is transferred as a gift to the trust, a gift tax will be charged.

Secrecy is always a key factor in these kinds of tax-haven transactions. Bermuda itself does not have a secrecy law, but the bank officer stressed that his financial dealings would always be carried out in complete confidentiality. The U.S. resident himself would have to be careful when it comes to correspondence, transfer of money, and conversations between friends and neighbors.

The Bermuda bank officer would not comment on whether setting up this kind of trust would be in violation of U.S. law. "The U.S. investor must seek his own legal counsel on this matter," he said. The U.S. resident relies primarily on secrecy, but if his scheme is discovered, he can argue that the trust arrangement is technically in accordance with the U.S. Tax Code because he is neither grantor, trustee, nor beneficiary of the trust.

What about the IRS position? Undoubtedly its attitude would not be favorable. It would argue that there is "no substance" to the "form" of the trust, that in fact the U.S. resident is the grantor because he puts money in the trust, and that he is the trustee because he gives investment instructions. The battle would be fought in Tax Court, and undoubtedly would be settled in favor of the IRS.

So, we're back to square one. Some U.S. investors, willing to take the chance, set up an offshore trust and depend on luck to keep the IRS from finding out about it. But when all is said and done, there is little difference between this and blatant tax evasion. Possibly you would avoid a criminal fraud case, but for this privilege, you'll pay several thousand dollars in administrative fees, which vary from trustee to trustee.

The Bahamas

The Commonwealth of the Bahamas is the tax haven closest to the U.S.; Nassau is only 200 miles east of Miami. The beaches, skin-diving, and other amenities are pleasant, though I would rank Bermuda ahead of the Bahamas when it comes to food and hospitality.

The black people are in control of the government. It has been more than a decade since blacks took over, and so far the relationship with Americans has been cordial. Tourist trade with the U.S. is substantial. Many investors are concerned, however, that the government will turn pro-communist, with Cuba being such a close neighbor, and turn against U.S. investors and tourists. Recently, the Bahamian government issued regulations denying foreigners the right to own real estate in the Bahamas for "speculative" purposes, creating a bear market for now. So far, there are no other indications of anti-U.S. attitudes.

The commonwealth is not party to any tax treaties, and has no direct taxes on income, capital gains, or estates. Because of its comprehensive bank secrecy law, many U.S. investors set up foreign trusts and corporations in the Bahamas.

I have visited Nassau on several occasions and have investigated the services of Bahamian banks and trust companies. Some of the more prestigious trust companies, such as the Roy West Trust Co., will no longer assist Americans because of the 1976 U.S. tax law. But many Bahamian-owned trust companies and banks continue to offer their services to Americans.

On one occasion I accompanied an acquaintance who wanted to set up an offshore trust. One trust company was particularly anxious to help. Its officers were well aware of the changes in the 1976 Tax

Reform Act, and they presented a trust document that could not be traced to the U.S. investor. Like the trust setup in Bermuda, this one did not list the U.S. resident as grantor, trustee, or beneficiary. But this trust arrangement went further. The trustee, which would be the Bahamian trust company, would be under no legal obligation to name you, your children, or anyone else as the beneficiaries. You could offer suggested beneficiaries, and the company would agree to consider them. Of course, the presumption was that the company would follow your recommendations completely, but technically it doesn't have to. Consequently, the Bahamian secret trust appeared to qualify as a trust exempt from U.S. taxation.

After the trust is established, other financial arrangements can be made to further reduce tax liabilities. The trust could form a foreign-based corporation in Panama, Hong Kong, or other countries that don't tax profits from sources outside the country. The corporation would be directed by bank nominees, so your name would not appear anywhere, although you would secretly be giving investment instructions. Thus, the Bahamian trust company is willing to set up a *double wall of secrecy* through the trust/corporation structure.

As you can see, trust and confidentiality are essential aspects of Bahamian trusts and corporations. If the trust company didn't follow your instructions or embezzled the funds, you would have little recourse. You certainly could not go through government channels to get your money back. The administrative costs for this tricky setup are less than in Bermuda, but you can still expect to pay several thousand dollars to organize the trust and corporation, and several more to maintain it. Is the reward worth the risk?

The Cayman Islands

When I visited the Cayman Islands, the people were bustling with activity. I met with several attorneys, management firm personnel, and bank officers. Swiss Bank Corporation is the only one of the big-three Swiss banks with a street branch in the Caymans. According to the Swiss Bank officer, the bank doesn't want trouble with the U.S. government because it has large holdings in the United States. Evidently other Swiss banks feel the same way.

There are several trust/corporation schemes at work in the Caymans, similar to those in the Bahamas. In one arrangement, a Cayman management firm sets up a Cayman corporation on the client's behalf using *bearer shares.* As you may know, bearer shares have no name attached to them, so that whoever possesses, or bears, the certificates is presumed to be the owner of the corporation. Like cash, bearer shares follow the axiom "Possession is nine-tenths of the law." The management firm then establishes a foreign trust in the Cayman Islands on behalf of the corporation, which holds the bearer shares. On paper, the U.S. citizen is neither the grantor, trustee, nor beneficiary of the trust. The beneficiary in this case is an international charity or foundation. The charity organization, however, is never made aware of the fact that it is the beneficiary, and in fact the money is never transferred from the corporation to the beneficiary, even after the U.S. citizen dies. Supposedly the corporate assets are then turned over to someone who was previously selected by the U.S. investor. Meanwhile, the corporation invests in a variety of investments tax-free; taxes are avoided because Cayman doesn't tax investments, and the U.S. doesn't tax the corporation because the U.S. investor doesn't appear to own the corporation.

How is money transferred to the bearer company? Transfers can be made by gift, but the $10,000-a-year gift exclusion is very limiting. In most cases, appreciated assets can be sold to the foreign corporation, which pays back the U.S. investors on an installment basis for low-tax advantages. Of course, this leaves a paper trail for the U.S. government to follow, and may lead to an IRS audit. But that's only one of the risks you take when participating in this kind of deal.

Why all this elaborate setup, costing from $2,000 to $7,500? The promoter of the above method suggested that this trust/corporation plan would withstand IRS scrutiny, especially when the beneficiary of the trust appears to be an international charitable organization like the Red Cross. And that's *if* the government finds out about it, he emphasized.

But the IRS does find out about these schemes. Undoubtedly it has investigated many of the Cayman management firms setting up these deals, or sent agents to attend the conferences sponsored by the management firms. The IRS has won numerous court cases showing that the technical formation of a legal entity doesn't matter so much as the intent of the U.S. investor. The "substance over form" principle has been upheld in numerous cases; if the U.S.

investor has ultimate control over the corporation, even if that control is from a respectable distance, the profits are currently taxable.

Nevertheless, because the IRS doesn't have the manpower to investigate everyone, Cayman Islands business continues to flourish. Secrecy and trust are important elements of tax-haven merchandising, and both are seldom breached.

Other Popular Tax Havens

There are, of course, dozens of other tax havens besides those in the Caribbean. Most are very small countries that depend on foreign investments. They include Panama, the Turks and Caicos, Curaçao, the British and U.S. Virgin Islands, Costa Rica, the Channel Islands, Monaco, the Isle of Man, Liechtenstein, Luxembourg, and many others.

Liechtenstein, a small country sandwiched between Switzerland and Austria, exemplifies the tax-haven activities in Europe. During a recent visit to Switzerland, I took a short trip by train to Vaduz, the capital of Liechtenstein. There are three major banks there and many law offices. Liechtenstein has no tax treaty with any country except Austria, and imposes no income, capital gains, or estate taxes on foreign companies established there.

I met with a well-known attorney who sets up trusts, corporations, and foundations in Liechtenstein. This country has a unique financial law that permits you to establish any kind of trust or corporation. The attorney described in detail the advantages of establishing a bearer *Anstalt,* whereby the person physically holding the "deed of assignment" is the owner. In this case, space for the name of the owner is left blank, thereby permitting the buyer to transfer the deed to someone else privately.

The most private type of financial organization in Liechtenstein is called the *stiftung* or "private foundation." Such private foundations are not required to be listed in the public registry. The Liechtenstein foundation cannot engage in any commercial business, but it can be an investment company. This type of company costs several thousand dollars to establish and even more to maintain. The attorney warned, quite candidly, that it would be difficult for Americans to take advantage of Liechtenstein's legal entities to avoid taxation.

NEGATIVE ON TAX HAVENS?

I have been rather negative on tax havens thus far, and for good reason. The establishment of secret foreign trusts, bearer corporations, and anonymous foundations can only lead to trouble in the long run because they rely too heavily on secrecy, and have all the appearances of a scheme. The reputation of many, though not all, of the promoters is also questionable. If you are taken advantage of and lose your money, you have no recourse. Moreover, you may spend some sleepless nights worrying that the IRS will discover your operation. You might avoid criminal fraud penalties, but civil fines, back taxes, and interest can be substantial if you lose in court.

POSITIVE USES OF TAX HAVENS

Are all tax-haven activities suspicious? Not at all! Most tax-haven business is designed to assist citizens of *other* nations that are exempt from taxation on offshore income. The problem for Americans arises from the fact that the United States is one of the few countries that taxes its citizens and its businesses no matter where they are domiciled. Consequently, the U.S. citizen is extremely limited in the kinds of offshore activities he can engage in that will result in the legal elimination or postponement of taxation.

What are some of the positive, albeit limited, ways in which Americans can do business or invest abroad tax-free? They include the following possibilities:

Equal Partners in Offshore Business

U.S. law provides for the postponement of taxes due on a foreign corporation, if at least half of it is owned by a foreigner or "nonresident alien." Thus, it's possible for you to escape taxation on a foreign corporation if you have a bona fide foreigner willing to become your full partner by putting up an equal share of capital. You must not have majority ownership of the foreign corporation.

I recently met a person who had established such a company. He was a U.S. citizen who had set up a foreign corporation, retaining 49% ownership. The other 51% of the stock was owned by an English expatriate living in Costa Rica. The U.S. investor had to file an information return with the IRS, so the business wasn't a secret to the U.S. government. But by law he did not have to pay any taxes on earnings or profits in the company because he didn't have majority ownership.

Taxes would only be due when he receives a dividend. And if he sells his shares of the foreign corporation, the gain would be 60% tax-free as a long-term capital gain.

Here was an unusual partnership of two compatible businessmen. Frankly, I think the only reason this exemption is still allowed in the tax code is that it is of such limited use to Americans. It is difficult enough to find a full partner willing to put up substantial capital to start a business without requiring that he be a foreigner. Another major drawback to this arrangement is the possible tax problems of the foreign investor. In many cases, he, too, must arrange his affairs so as to avoid his own country's taxes. Ideally, the best partner would be someone who has become an expatriate from his own country, thereby avoiding taxation altogether. In the case above, the partner was an English expatriate, and therefore was not subject to British levies. Fortunately, there are some countries that, like America, do not tax income from foreign corporations where citizens are not majority holders. A 50-50 partnership, wherein neither party has majority ownership, is ideal.

The 11-Partner Rule

Another exemption involves the establishment of a foreign corporation with 11 or more equal shareholders. Under this arrangement, the law states that 11 or more U.S. residents can be shareholders in a foreign corporation and avoid current taxation on corporate earnings, as long as no dividend is declared. Dividends would be taxed as ordinary income.

Again, this is an example that has limited appeal. Finding 11 or more like-minded investors to set up a foreign corporation is difficult, although not impossible. The 11 shareholders cannot be "related persons," so you could not have a family-owned foreign corporation.

Offshore Banking

Offshore banking is an exception to the 11-partner rule. A U.S. investor can set up his own bank in a tax haven, engage in the foreign banking business, and defer U.S. taxes on undistributed profits. This little-known exception has been extremely profitable for major U.S. corporations and wealthy individuals who have established their own offshore banks.

The most popular offshore banking centers have been the tax havens—the Bahamas, the Cayman Islands, the Netherlands Antilles, Hong Kong, Montserrat, Panama, and the Turks and Caicos. These financial centers generally impose no income or capital gains taxes on foreign banks, although they do require annual licensing fees. Recently most of the tax havens have raised the minimum paid-in capital needed to qualify for a banking license to almost $1 million, making it difficult to establish an offshore bank unless you are already a wealthy investor or a major corporation. One reason for this is that there were many scandals surrounding the establishment of "post-office banks" by shady characters in St. Vincent and other Caribbean Islands in the mid-1970s. There are still a few offbeat places that offer low capital requirements to start a bank, but fees and minimums change constantly.

Foreign banks controlled by U.S. citizens must be careful if they wish to avoid U.S. taxation and regulation. They should not have an office in the U.S., nor should they advertise or solicit customers there or in any other way engage in the banking trade in the U.S. Otherwise, U.S. regulators could claim that the foreign bank is an unlicensed bank, or that the foreign bank is subject to U.S. taxation because it is engaged in U.S. trade or business.

The most conservative approach would be to solicit business from foreigners living outside the U.S. The bank could advertise in foreign publications, including the English-speaking *International Herald Tribune* and the international editions of *Time* and *Newsweek*.

Controlled foreign banks must also act like banks. It would be a mistake for a U.S. investor to establish an offshore bank solely for his personal use, just to avoid taxes. The IRS would regard this as a "personal holding company," making it subject to taxation. A foreign bank should accept deposits, make loans, invest in the Eurocurrency market, offer trust services, and consult with clients. Unlike U.S. banks, a foreign bank can buy and sell securities, commodities, and other investments on behalf of the bank and its clients. Any interest, dividends, or capital gains earned by the bank would be free of U.S. tax.

Foreign Investments

Certain kinds of investments can still be made overseas without incurring any current tax liability. These investments largely involve non-income-producing assets, such as:

— Gold and silver (coins or bullion) warehoused in Europe, Latin America, or Asia.
— Real estate, such as raw land, a house, or a condominium. Rental income is taxable if you lease the property or rent the condo, but, as with domestic real estate, capital gains are not taxed until the property is sold.
— Stored commodities, such as strategic metals, vintage wines, stamps, fine art, and other collectibles.

Until you sell these investments, any paper profits you earn are untaxed. If you hold these investments for at least a year, you can take a long-term capital gain, 60% tax-free, when you sell. Thus, in most cases, the rules for investing abroad are the same as for U.S. based investing.

There are some exceptions that tax-haven experts have uncovered in the tax code. For example, it's still possible for a foreign company to buy and sell delivered commodities and postpone taxes until the money is repatriated to the United States. The creation of this foreign entity must be "properly structured" (a key phrase in all international tax planning) in order to take advantage of this exemption.

Offshore income-producing investments also have some benefits. You can avoid current taxation on foreign-currency annuities and endowments. Swiss annuities have been extremely popular for American retirees. Swiss endowment policies offer a good long-term investment in Swiss francs while deferring taxes on the interest and dividends. Once you start receiving the foreign annuity, the interest and dividend portion is taxable. But until then, there is total deferral.

CHOOSING A TAX-HAVEN SPECIALIST

I have been purposely vague in many areas of foreign-haven activity for several reasons. First, the legalities are extremely complex; lengthy books have been written about the details of international financial planning. I have therefore given only a broad outline of what's available.

Setting up a trust or corporation offshore is expensive, costing several thousand dollars a year. No investor should consider using a foreign haven unless he expects to place at least $100,000 abroad initially. My opinion is that the costs are definitely inflated, which offsets part of your tax savings.

Finally, I have not recommended any tax-haven specialists by name because of their necessity for a low profile. This is not to say that there aren't any capable attorneys or accountants that specialize in overseas tax planning. On the contrary, I have met personally with several. But most of them don't want or need the notoriety of having their names and services publicized in a book.

One tax attorney told me that many professional tax experts are working full-time for their wealthy clients on legitimate offshore projects—"all well within the legal framework," he said. "Stay away from shady deals in secret trusts and bearer corporations," he warned. I asked if he would be willing to take on any additional clients, and he responded candidly, "Not now. . . . I hardly have the time to care for the projects I've already started."

There are legitimate tax-shelter opportunities still available overseas, put together by top professionals for their wealthy clients. Loopholes still exist in the U.S. Tax Code, despite the 1976 Tax Reform Act and other efforts by Congress to close deferral techniques. Few of these methods are revealed on paper, nor are the real professionals tempted to promote them publicly to unseen novices. This fact should serve as a warning: Stay away from promoters of tax-haven deals that promise tax-free investing, charging $10,000 to reveal their "secret plan."

Legal specialists will reveal little on paper. At best, they may write a private memorandum for a client's eyes only. The last thing a tax attorney wants is publicity. The government doesn't mind a loophole that drains little from potential revenues, but it becomes deeply concerned when a loophole becomes so popular that billions of dollars escape taxation. That's why commodity tax straddles were nixed by Congress—the government was losing an estimated $4 billion a year in potential revenues because of them. Whenever a tax ploy becomes too popular, the IRS and Congress get tough, challenging the technique or changing the law entirely.

Sometimes, Congress deliberately writes loopholes into the law.

In the case of tax havens, certain entities are intentionally exempt from current taxation, such as foreign corporations half owned by nonresident aliens, or owned by 11 or more U.S. investors. But there's another kind of loophole that tax experts are always looking for. This is truly a loophole, not an intentional exemption. Usually Congress simply didn't think about it when it wrote the law. A slight change in technical language can alter the meaning of the law, creating a loophole out of semantics. Despite the intent of the law, these technical exceptions are perfectly within the fair interpretation of the law. This is the kind of loophole many professionals are seeking.

FINDING AN ADVISER

There are probably several hundred attorneys and accountants across the country who specialize in foreign operations. They are generally located in major cities. Some are more aggressive than others, so you must find an expert compatible with your own approach to taxes.

What kind of tax-haven adviser should you be looking for? An accountant or CPA may have an excellent grasp of the highly technical financial arrangements that might be involved. A general financial adviser who specializes in tax havens may offer a wider range of international tax planning.

My recommendation, however, is to use a *tax attorney*. Client privilege is extremely important in setting up offshore activities. As one specialist told me, "Every client I have has asked about client privilege. I think it's very important, and I believe it's a mistake for any investor interested in tax havens to rely on an accountant or tax adviser. He must use an attorney for complete confidentiality, since an accountant or adviser has no client privilege in a court of law, if it ever came down to that." This is not to imply that anything shady is taking place. It simply means that an investor must feel uninhibited in his quest for the best planning possible—and he should not feel restricted in his ability to ask the widest degree of questions about his offshore operations. An area as technical as tax havens for U.S. citizens can never be completely black and white—there is a great deal of gray that is subject to various interpretations by private or government legal authorities.

If you are interested in an offshore presence, I would recommend that you first seek competent legal counsel or financial specialists in your area. Make some appointments and determine with whom you would feel most comfortable as your adviser in this field.

SUMMARY: TREAD CAREFULLY IN TAX HAVENS

There are both positive and negative factors affecting your decision to invest or do business offshore. Don't become so concerned about privacy and tax freedom that you ignore sound business tactics. Be alert to excessive costs. Stay clear of dubious offshore schemes that emphasize only secrecy and mutual trust. Use only top-notch specialists in the field. And, most important, make sure your program is legally sound.

It is important that you know your subject, so that you do not have to rely entirely on the interpretations of others. For a conservative approach to tax havens, I recommend these two publications:

Practical International Tax Planning, by Marshall J. Langer (Practising Law Institute, 810 Seventh Ave., New York, NY 10019; $40).
The Robert Kinsman Guide to Tax Havens (Dow Jones–Irwin, Homewood, IL 60430; $17.50).

Problem Solver #5

Q. Several years ago when I was serving in the army I met a German citizen. We became the best of friends, and have kept in touch. Since meeting, we have both become successful businessmen. Now he writes and says he has some money he would like to invest in the United States. How can I help?

A. You have a golden opportunity to set up a tax-free foreign corporation! You should definitely consider joining together and forming an offshore investment company in a tax haven. Each of you should be willing to put up the same amount of capital. As long as you do not own a majority interest in the foreign corporation, you do not have to pay any U.S. income taxes on the corporation's profits.

If you sell your shares in the corporation, or the corporation declares a dividend, you would have to pay taxes. Otherwise, the foreign investment company can keep growing and expanding completely tax-free. Your foreign corporation could purchase a resort condominium, Treasury bills, bank certificates of deposit, gold and silver, South African gold shares, mutual funds, growth stocks, collectibles, etc. You can earn high interest and receive tax-free dividends. You can trade the markets aggressively, including futures and options, without paying taxes; this is a great way to build a fortune.

7

─How to Beat Social Security

SOCIAL SECURITY can be added to politics, sports, and religion as a topic to be avoided in polite conversation.

Mention the growing burden it presents to an American over 45, and he will become indignant: "I've paid into the system all my life. It's no handout, I've earned my pension!" Mention that same argument to someone under 40, and the reaction will be just as indignant: "I'm paying more in social security taxes than I do in income taxes, and it all goes directly to someone else's benefit check. By the time I'm 65, there won't be anything left!" Politicians defend their retired constituents by saying, "We've made a commitment to the elderly and America will not renege on her promises!" A few observers respond, "What right do we have to make impossible promises that will have to be kept by our grandchildren?"

Social security is a serious problem facing our country. Originally established to provide *supplemental* retirement income at a time when the average life span was 61 years, it has become, in many cases, the *only* source of income for retirees who are living longer and retiring earlier. Social security benefits are tied to the cost of living and are increasing rapidly. Medicare and Medicaid have been added to supplement "inadequate" benefits.

Social security is called a pension plan, when in fact, not long ago, the Supreme Court stated that it is nothing more than a *welfare* system. Social security is *not* a bona fide pension program. A pension plan takes the money invested by workers and keeps it in a trust fund that invests in long-term investments. Through wise man-

100

agement, compounding of interest, and tax deferral, a worker's original savings multiply until, by retirement, he has amassed enough money to live comfortably the rest of his life.

Social security benefits are paid in just the opposite manner. Money is paid to current beneficiaries the minute it is received. There is no long-term investing of funds. Moreover, benefits are essentially unrelated to how much you put into the program. A person who has paid into the system a minimum 10 years (40 quarters) qualifies for the same monthly payments as someone who has paid into the program all his life.

With proponents now talking of borrowing from general funds to pay for social security, it is no wonder that younger workers are complaining that by the time they reach retirement age there will be nothing left except a mountain of debt.

Social security, like other federal welfare schemes, began with an extremely low budget. In 1937, workers and employers paid a mere 1% each on the first $1,000 of income. Since then it has grown into a monster. In 1982, both employer and employee pay 6.7% on all income up to $32,400. That means that the average worker will pay over $1,000 in social security, or FICA, taxes this year. Considering that the employer must contribute an equal amount, the actual "contribution" comes to over $2,000.

Self-employed individuals pay in 1982 a rate of 9.35% on $32,400, or a maximum tax of over $3,000!

This base salary is tied to the cost of living, so as wages go up, FICA liabilities go up. If current figures aren't staggering enough, consider the fact that just ten years from now it is estimated that a worker earning $60,000 a year will pay 15% of his income to social security, amounting to $9,000!

THE SOLUTION TO SOCIAL SECURITY

How can this madness be stopped? So far, all efforts to reduce benefits have been stalemated by a Congress overly sensitive to the retirement community. Retirees represent the largest voting block in the country, and are the group with the highest percentage of active voters. And as long as benefits are linked to the cost of living, this influential group of constituents will bring little real pressure on Congress to lower the inflation rate.

Meanwhile, there are increasing efforts to boost the revenues used to pay for social security. Some advocates call for making the program mandatory for *all* workers, including federal employees, who currently enjoy the benefits of a separate, well-run pension plan. Others advocate doing away with the exemption on earnings above the wage base (presently $32,400), a soak-the-rich scheme that would require employers and employees to pay a percentage of *total* income. This would greatly increase tax liabilities without increasing benefits.

Several years ago a presidential candidate suggested that social security be made voluntary for workers under 40 years of age. To me, this seems like a good start. The old system could be phased out gradually, without harming those who are already approaching retirement, and be replaced by far superior private pension programs that have already proved their successfulness.

I do not believe that we should make any alternative pension plan mandatory, however. That's one of the chief stumbling blocks with social security—people are being forced to enter a long-term savings program that ignores their current needs. True, those who don't plan ahead might find themselves unable to retire when they want to, but the freedom to fail is just as important as the freedom to succeed. I believe that if people are allowed the widest possible choices on how to spend and save their money, they will ultimately make the right decisions.

But while I do not favor mandatory pension plans, I do favor tax incentive programs such as Keogh or individual retirement accounts. Contributions to these funds are tax-deductible, and earnings within the pension program are tax-free until they are withdrawn, providing a strong motivation to save. There is also a penalty for withdrawing your money before retirement, which encourages long-term savings. Significantly, you are not required by law to participate.

This principle of tax-favored private pension plans is now well established, and is already a supplement to social security. Efforts should be made to allow these pension plans to phase social security out gradually before it reaches total bankruptcy. This is the only real solution to the massive welfare dilemma we're facing in this country.

Needless to say, I don't expect this to happen. I expect social security to get deeper into trouble, doing irreparable damage to our economy. It is the Achilles' heel and fatal flaw of our economic system.

SHOULD YOU GET OUT?

Should you try to escape social security through the exemptions outlined in this chapter? What benefits, if any, would you forfeit? What if you've paid into FICA for decades, and you suddenly stop paying—would you lose benefits?

Social security has a number of benefits besides a tax-free guaranteed monthly retirement income that is tied to the cost of living. Other advantages include:

1. *Survivors insurance.* Full monthly payments to your widow if 60 years or older, or disabled widow, 50–59; widow regardless of age who has children under 18 or full-time students; dependent children, dependent widower if 62 years or older; and a lump-sum death payment.
2. *Disability insurance.* Full monthly payments if you become permanently or partially disabled.
3. *Hospital insurance.* Under Medicare, general hospital coverage up to 60 days, and sometimes longer, for people over 65 years old.

Generally, most people have to work a minimum 10 years (40 quarters) to qualify for full insurance under social security. These years do not have to be consecutive. However, workers who do not enter the work force until after 55 are required to work fewer years to fully qualify.

But let's face it. Most people aren't worried about qualifying— they already qualified years ago, and are still waiting to collect. Meanwhile, they continue to pay ever higher FICA premiums. Therefore, it would be to the individual's advantage to stop paying into social security without disqualifying himself from future benefits. Believe it or not, this is possible.

There are a surprising number of ways to opt out of social security. Nearly 10% of U.S. workers are not covered by social security. The easiest way to avoid future social security taxes is simply to switch to a job that does not require social security participation. You still qualify for social security at retirement, but you don't pay any more into the system. Perhaps one or more of the following exemptions will apply to your situation.

PUBLIC WORKERS AVOID SOCIAL SECURITY

One of the most ironic exemptions to social security is the exemption for federal workers.

For example, the congressmen who created and perpetuate the social security mess do not pay into it. Nor do the congressmen's staff. Not only do they avoid paying the FICA tax, but the regular federal pension program is optional to congressmen and their staffs. Working for Congress can be an extremely rewarding and valuable experience, and there are several thousand jobs available on "the Hill." Since a national election occurs every two years, the turnover of jobs is very high, offering you a better chance of landing a job for your representative, or for any representative.

Federal civilian employees, numbering 2.8 million across the country, are exempt from social security taxes. Even more ironic is the fact that employees of the Social Security Administration do not pay into the system they run! They have a generous pension program of their own. The federal employee pays 7% of his base income, which is matched by the government. The benefits of the federal pension program far exceed those of social security—some estimates show that the guaranteed monthly income for the average federal retiree exceeds social security payments by two to three times!

Other quasi-public workers also have their own pension programs, e.g., employees of the Federal Reserve System, the Comptroller of the Currency, and the U.S. Postal Service.

Some state and local government workers (including public-school teachers) don't pay into social security. The decision, however, must be made at the administrative level, not by the individual employee. If a state or city government decides to drop out of social security, *all* employees become exempt. But if the local government decides to stay in, employees have no choice but to pay FICA taxes. The federal government must be given two years' notice before a local government can leave the system, and social security must be replaced by an alternative pension plan, based on sound actuarial principles. Sometimes the public authority permits a variety of investment alternatives, similar to the "teacher's annuity." The most recent example of a government unit leaving social security is the entire state of Alaska.

TAX-EXEMPT FOUNDATIONS CAN AVOID SOCIAL SECURITY

Few people realize that nonprofit organizations are automatically exempt from social security taxes, and federal unemployment taxes, unless they sign a "waiver certificate" (Form SS-15), which waives this exemption and allows employees of the foundation to become participants in social security.

A tax-exempt foundation is an organization established for charitable, religious, scientific, or educational purposes. Nonprofit organizations number close to a million in the United States, and they employ several million Americans. A recent study by the Council on Foundations reported that only 6% of all private grant-making foundations do not belong to social security, but the percentage is probably higher for public foundations, charities, and churches. The number opting out of social security could increase dramatically over the next few years as more tax-exempt organizations realize that they don't have to participate. It would be worthwhile contacting foundations in your area for job opportunities. *The National Directory of Addresses and Telephone Numbers* (Concord Reference Books, 14 Park Rd., Tinton Falls, NJ 07724; $19.95) gives a listing of major foundations around the country; for a complete listing, see your local library.

THE RELIGIOUS EXEMPTION

The religious exemption to social security has been popularized recently by the growing tax revolt, but it does not have the great potential for beating the system that many had hoped.

There are two legitimate religious exemptions. The first one is somewhat curious and applies only to small sects. This is IRS Form 4029, "Application for Exemption from Tax on Self-Employment Income and Waiver of Benefits." Members of certain religious groups, such as the Amish, can be exempt from the self-employment tax if they waive their rights to all benefits. They must be members of a "recognized religious group" which, as a group, is conscientiously opposed to social security. They must never have received social security in the past. In addition, they must be opposed to *any* private insurance plan! Needless to say, this isn't the kind of exemption that many people would want to qualify for.

A much more successful method has been to file Form 4361, "Application for Exemption from Self-Employment Tax for Use by Ministers, Members of Religious Orders and Christian Science Practitioners." Ministers can take an *irrevocable* exemption from social security if they are conscientiously opposed to it. They cannot reverse this decision someday in the future. The waiver must be filed at the beginning of service, and it applies only to religious earnings. Private pension plans are allowed.

A few tax-revolt groups have attempted to set up religious orders to take advantage of the exemption, but obviously this method does not work if you're an employee of a company that withholds FICA taxes, or when you are self-employed in nonreligious endeavors.

THE SUBCHAPTER S DEVICE

Income from dividends or interest is exempt from social security taxes. Some investors and businessmen have taken advantage of this fact by setting up a Subchapter S corporation. Under this corporate structure, all profits from the corporation are passed on to the shareholders as dividend income, without paying corporate income taxes. Shareholders have to pay income taxes on the dividend income, but not FICA taxes.

One of the problems with this arrangement is that your Subchapter S corporation does not pay you a salary. If you are audited, the IRS could argue that such a technique is merely a tax-avoidance ploy, and that your dividends are, in reality, a salary. FICA taxes would be imposed accordingly. Some auditors may allow the exemption, others may not. It is certainly not a surefire way to beat social security.

OVERSEAS AMERICANS CAN AVOID SOCIAL SECURITY

A U.S. citizen employed outside the country by a foreign business can avoid U.S. social security taxes, but it is likely that he will be required to pay into the social security program of the foreign government. Many tax havens, discussed in previous chapters, have no employee-funded social programs, however, so you could successfully avoid social security payments in either country.

Closer to home, such international organizations as the World Bank or the United Nations do not impose social security taxes on their U.S.-based employees, a unique advantage.

A self-employed American can avoid the self-employment tax on his earnings by working abroad, provided he does not exceed the income exemption level ($75,000 in 1982). He must also be a bona fide resident of a foreign country.

THE FAMILY BUSINESS

Special exemptions have been provided for a family business or partnership. The following situations avoid social security taxes:

— a wife employed by husband
— a husband employed by wife
— a child under 21 years of age employed by parent(s)

The exemptions apply to foster children and stepchildren, as well as to adopted children.

One person in the family—the owner of the company—still has to pay the self-employment tax. But the spouse and children working for the company are exempt from FICA taxes. This is a tremendous savings. The only requirement is that the business must withhold federal income taxes from the salaries of the family employees.

Be careful in setting up your business that it fully complies with all regulations. For example, if the husband and wife are both listed on your annual tax return as *co-owners,* you could be liable for *double self-employment taxes,* amounting to 18.7% of your profits! The IRS might argue that if both spouses are running the business, they are co-owners and should each pay the self-employment tax. To avoid this problem, be sure to list only one spouse as the owner, and the other spouse as an employee. To emphasize this distinction, only the owner should have signature authority on the company checks.

A corporation does not qualify for the family-business exemption. In a corporate status, all employees, including children and spouse, are subject to FICA withholding. Only single proprietorships and family partnerships avoid the social security tax on related parties. The family partnership must include only the husband and wife— no other family members or relatives may be involved as partners.

THE UNEARNED-INCOME EXCLUSION

Dividends and interest are exempt from both FICA taxation and federal unemployment taxes. There are other forms of "unearned" income that are also exempt. Capital gains are exempt, unless your investment activities constitute a business or trade. Income from a trust, retirement and pension payments, and rental income from residential or commercial property are all normally exempt.

Royalties are usually exempt from social security, but book royalties are an uncertain area. If the author is not engaged primarily in the business of bookwriting, he is exempt. If, on the other hand, the author writes several books, or prepares new editions of the same book, the IRS argues that the author must pay social security on his royalties.

THE STUDENT EXEMPTION

In many cases, full-time or part-time students may be exempt from social security and unemployment taxes. For example, students working for a *private* school, college, or university can avoid the FICA tax. However, students working for a public educational institution would normally be taxed, unless the public school or college is in a state which has opted out of the social security system.

OTHER LITTLE-KNOWN EXCLUSIONS

There are many other little-known exclusions to social security which are of limited use to the average American. For example:

— deliverers of newspapers or advertising material other than magazines, who are under 18 years of age

— foreign agricultural workers hired on a temporary basis
— nonresident aliens temporarily working in the U.S.
— noncash payments for domestic workers and housekeepers

Businessmen should know that you can pay a part-time worker up to $400 each year without having to pay or withhold social security.

In addition, you can hire "temporaries" from a temporary agency without paying their employment taxes, even if you hire them for a lengthy period of time. Of course, you pay *indirectly* because the temporary agency is required to withhold for the temporaries, and the wage rate reflects that expense. But you do avoid the paperwork and hassle of withholding.

CONCLUSION: YOU CAN BEAT SOCIAL SECURITY

As we have seen, there are many ways to escape the onerous social security tax. The best technique is to switch your current employment to one that does not require participation in social security (federal jobs, nonprofit organizations, etc.), or to work overseas. Obviously, you should seek out employment that has many rewards other than tax benefits, but if you are currently in the job market it would be worthwhile to investigate some of these alternatives.

Problem Solver #6

Q. I am in my early thirties, earning a decent income, but I'm sick and tired of paying more and more for social security, especially knowing that the system is going bankrupt, and there probably won't be anything left when I retire at 65. Is there any way I can get out?

A. Well, I won't recommend that you become an ordained minister or move to Alaska! But there are some practical steps you can take. There are 30 million Americans who don't have to pay into social security every year—from federal and state workers to employees of nonprofit organizations. There are a lot of job opportunities out there. Start searching immediately for a fulfilling job that doesn't require participation in social security.

If you have the entrepreneur spirit, consider setting up your own tax-exempt educational or scientific foundation, and pay yourself a salary, free of social security. Or set up a small corporation that pays a very small salary, thus minimizing what you have to pay in FICA taxes.

8

— Maximum Profits from Your Pension Plan

YOU MUST look beyond social security if you hope to have financial independence in your mature years. A well-rounded investment portfolio, consisting of stocks, bonds, precious metals, real estate, and money market instruments, will, of course, play a key role in preserving your standard of living.

In addition, the establishment of a large retirement fund is absolutely essential. Recent legislation has vastly expanded the advantages of setting up a retirement program. In fact, it's now possible to have *several* tax-deferred pension plans. Most individuals can participate in either a corporate pension plan or a self-employed Keogh plan, and they can have an Individual Retirement Account (IRA) as well.

PENSION PLANS: PROS AND CONS

There are many tax benefits to be derived from IRS-approved pension plans for those who are in high tax brackets.

First, income placed in a pension plan is not taxed on your current return. Theoretically, you are in a higher tax bracket in your earning years than you will be after retirement, so your tax liability on the money you have set aside will be lower when you begin withdrawing it.

For this reason, you should not consider putting money into a pension plan until you have reached the 30% tax bracket. Otherwise, it's quite possible that you will be in a higher tax bracket when you start withdrawing your funds, and you'll end up owing more, not less.

Second, interest, dividends, and capital gains earned in your pension are not currently taxed. Thus, the full amount continues to increase in value at a compounded rate.

Third, if you should die before retirement, the benefits would be free from federal estate taxes and gift taxes if paid to a named beneficiary other than the "estate."

Of course, there are disadvantages, too. There are withdrawal penalties and immediate tax liabilities if you take your money out before retirement, which is defined presently as age 59½ for Keogh and IRA accounts. The early-withdrawal penalty is currently 10%.

Another important consideration is that all withdrawals—whether coming from original principal, interest, dividends, or capital gains—will be treated as "ordinary income" on your tax return. If you put long-term capital investments into your retirement fund, you will lose the 60% tax-free advantage.

Now let's take a look at each of these pension possibilities.

CORPORATE PENSION PLANS OFFER GREATEST BENEFITS

Corporate pension plans are extremely flexible, giving you the opportunity to make greater contributions than you would with a Keogh or IRA plan. In fact, corporate pension contributions have no specific dollar limitation, although annual payouts at retirement are limited by the IRS. There is no age limitation for withdrawing retirement pay, as there is for Keoghs or IRAs.

One type of plan, called the "money purchase pension plan," combines profit sharing with definite contributions and allows employees to set aside up to 25% of their salaries in the pension program. Another plan, called the "defined benefit pension plan," defines your retirement benefits first, and then determines how much you will need to contribute to the pension fund to meet the retirement goal. This sometimes results in tax-deductible contributions of 100% of one's salary, and is particularly beneficial to older participants who plan on retiring soon.

Andrew Westhem, a CLU and corporate pension expert from Beverly Hills, Calif., gives several examples. A 45-year-old who wanted to retire in 17 years could earn a salary of $40,000 a year and contribute $40,000 annually into a defined-benefit plan. If he was earning $120,000 a year, he could make an annual contribution of $90,000 to his plan. In the case of a 52-year-old earning $100,000 a year, he could contribute up to $150,000 to a defined-benefit plan! So you can see that you can shelter a great deal of income through a corporate pension program.

Unlike Keoghs or IRAs, corporate pension plans can be written to allow you to borrow against your funds. Restrictions vary, but some plans permit you to borrow as much as $50,000 or 50% of your equity in the pension's assets, whichever is less. Use this borrowed money for further investments, such as income-producing real estate, and your retirement money will provide double service for you.

One of the exciting features of a corporate plan is that, as director of your own corporation, you can be *your own trustee.* This is one of the reasons that many self-employed individuals decide to incorporate. Keoghs and IRAs usually require a bank or other trustee to invest for you. But in a corporate pension program, you can be the trustee and make investments yourself. Your choice of investments is unlimited—choose between stocks, bonds, mutual funds, gold and silver, real estate, and even collectibles, since the ban on collectibles, as required in the 1981 tax law, does not apply to trustees in corporate plans. You can actually write the checks and make the deposits yourself.

You can also be the *custodian* of your own corporate pension plan. If you wish to hold collectibles, such as fine art, as part of your pension portfolio—and display them in your own home or at corporate headquarters—you can do so. You can also deposit coins, stamps, or stock certificates in your corporate office safe or safe deposit box. If you fear an economic or banking crisis sometime in the future, having tangible investments stored in your home or office may give you a greater sense of security.

Of course, not all corporate pension plans work this way. Many corporate officers prefer to turn their pension plans over to an independent trustee, such as a bank trust department, so they do not have to worry about choosing wise investments. But the choice is completely yours. If you have a corporate pension plan that does not have the features outlined above, perhaps you should make some changes, or get a new accountant or attorney to help you make the changes.

KEOGH PLANS: MORE BENEFITS, LOWEST COST

Many financial advisers tell their self-employed clients that setting up a corporation with a corporate pension plan is the only way to achieve maximum tax-deferrable contributions. Yet the costs of incorporating cannot be overlooked—there are attorneys' fees, higher social security taxes and unemployment compensation, and an incessant flow of government forms and fees. On the other hand, fringe-benefit packages are more enticing for corporations in terms of group insurance and pension plans. Each businessman and investor should weigh carefully the advantages and disadvantages of incorporating.

For many people, remaining an unincorporated proprietorship may be a better solution. You may not be eligible for the biggest fringe-benefit packages, but your costs will stay low. This is particularly true for a family business, which avoids employment taxes on spouse and children. Moreover, you can set up a Keogh plan for yourself and each of your employees, contributing 15% of their salaries or wages to the company Keogh plan, up to a maximum annual contribution of $15,000. The 1982 tax law increases the Keogh contributions to 20% of salary or $30,000 in 1984. Through wise portfolio management, this could result in a very generous retirement program.

It is also possible to set up a "defined benefit" Keogh plan, which will allow you to contribute more than 15% of your employees' salaries and wages to the retirement fund. This kind of plan defines the benefits desired at retirement first, and then determines the amount that must be contributed to assure those benefits.

INDIVIDUAL RETIREMENT ACCOUNTS (IRAs): SOMETHING FOR EVERYBODY

One of the most important changes in the 1981 tax law is that now every U.S. citizen can set up a tax-free Individual Retirement Account (IRA). Even if you are already a participant in a government or corporate pension plan, or have a self-employment Keogh, you can still set up an IRA.

In 1982, the 15%-of-salary limitation of IRA contributions was replaced by a straight maximum of $2,000. If a nonworking spouse is included in the IRA, the maximum is $2,250. If both spouses work, they can each put $2,000 into separate IRAs, making a total family contribution of $4,000. Contributions must come from earned income, i.e., wages or salary.

Children who have earned income can also have IRAs, but I strongly oppose this idea. Despite the recommendations of some financial advisers, there are several reasons why an IRA is *not* a good way to start a child's long-term savings program, particularly if it is intended to pay for his college education. First, a child can already earn up to $2,300 in wages and $1,000 in interest or dividends without paying any federal income taxes, so there is no advantage in placing $2,000 each year in a child's IRA. Second, a 10% penalty would be made on withdrawals used to pay for your child's college education, unless he plans to wait until he's 59½! Whenever the money is withdrawn it will be taxable income, taxes he wouldn't have paid had he *not* had an IRA!

Individual Retirement Accounts will, no doubt, become extremely popular over the next few years, with contributions increasing to far beyond the current $2,000 annual limitation. Millions of Americans will wisely take advantage of it.

SELF-DIRECTED PENSION PLANS

What's the best way to maximize your profits in a pension plan, whether it be a corporate plan, a Keogh, or an IRA?

My recommendation is to set up a *self-directed* plan, whereby *you* control the investment decisions. Get a trustee who will give you the widest variety of choices. Shop around. In the past, most people would simply open an IRA or Keogh at their local bank, with investment selections limited to the bank's own products, mostly low-yielding certificates of deposit.

This has all changed now. Many banks offer the opportunity to invest in practically anything, from bank CDs to stocks and bonds, charging a percentage or flat fee for their services. Bank fees differ greatly, so it pays to shop around. The most reasonable rates I've

How to Compare Retirement Plans

	Individual Retirement Account (IRA)	Self-Employed Retirement Account (Keogh)	Corporate Plan
How much can you contribute annually?	100% of salary up to $2,000; $250 may be added for unemployed spouse; employed spouse may set up separate IRA of up to $2,000.	15% of salary up to $15,000; in a defined contribution Keogh, you can contribute up to $30,000. Contributions increase to 20% of salary up to $30,000 in 1984.	Under a *defined contribution plan*, any combination of profit sharing or money purchase plan results in a maximum contribution of 25% of salary up to $45,475. Under a *defined benefit plan*, there is no specific dollar limitation. Whatever is actuarily necessary to fund a plan is allowed. *Example:* A 45-year-old earning $40,000 annually and retiring at 62 may have a $40,000 annual contribution to his plan!
What can you invest in?	Stocks, bonds, mutual funds, annuities, bank certificates, etc. No collectibles allowed. Can be self-directed.	Same as IRA: can be self-directed.	Small corporate plans can be self-directed; you serve as your own trustee. Prudent-man rule very liberal. Collectibles allowed if you are the trustee.
Can you borrow from the plan?	No.	No.	Yes, within limits.
When can you withdraw money for retirement?	No earlier than age 59½; 10% penalty applies unless totally disabled.	Same as IRA.	As early as age 62, depending on your plan.
How are withdrawals taxed?	All withdrawals are taxed at ordinary income rates. 5-year income averaging rules apply.	All withdrawals are taxed at ordinary income rates. But you can use special 10-year averaging on lump sum.	Same as Keogh, 10-year averaging on lump sum.

Courtesy: The Westol Company, 9665 Wilshire Blvd., Los Angeles, CA 90212 seen are available from Plymouth-Home National Bank (34 School St., Brockton, MA 02403), which charges only 2/5th of 1% per annum for administering your self-directed Keogh or IRA. Most banks typically charge around 1% per annum.

Brokerage Houses

Banks are not the only institutions offering IRAs and Keoghs. Perhaps the widest choice of investments is available from major brokerage houses, all of which offer self-directed Keoghs and IRAs. You can buy virtually any stock or bond on the market, as well as shares in money market funds and other mutual funds. Compare the annual fees carefully—they differ widely from firm to firm. Commissions can be a problem. Brokers will often recommend "load" mutual funds, from which the broker is paid a commission of 4–8½%, over "no-load" mutual funds, from which the broker gets nothing except goodwill.

One way of avoiding commission hungry brokers is by using a discount broker. Discount brokerage firms have also entered the Keogh and IRA market. They charge very little for commissions, as low as $25 per trade, and some charge next to nothing for annual administrative fees. Stockcross (1 Washington Mall, Boston, MA 02108; 800-225-6196), for instance, charges only $25 a year in annual fees to administer a Keogh or IRA.

Mutual Funds: The Best for the Least?

Mutual funds themselves may offer the least costly way to self-direct your pension plan. Many of the no-load funds charge no annual fee for administering your pension plan. They are set up to handle Keoghs, IRAs, corporate plans, 403(b) plans for employees of schools ("teacher's annuities"), hospitals, municipalities, and charitable organizations.

There are about 250 mutual funds in the United States. To see what they offer, I suggest you get a copy of the No-Load Mutual Fund Directory, which is available for $1 from: The No-Load Mutual Fund Association, Valley Forge, PA 19481. This directory lists most of the no-load mutual funds, including those investing in money market securities, growth stocks, bonds, gold shares, etc.

Vanguard, Fidelity, Scudder, Rowe-Price, Dreyfus, and other "family funds" offer a tremendous variety of investments to pension fund directors. You can switch from among a dozen funds or more, without charge, and by telephone. This allows you to take advantage of changing markets quickly and easily.

Fidelity's Group of Mutual Funds (82 Devonshire St., Boston, MA 02109; 800-225-6190, or in Mass., 617-726-0650) charges only $10 a year to maintain your pension program. You have your choice of 15 no-load mutual funds, which include a money market fund, a corporate bond fund, a government bond fund, an aggressive growth stock fund, etc. It also includes Fidelity's new "Select Portfolios" fund, which features individual portfolios in gold shares, high technology, energy, and health. Using Fidelity's toll-free number, you can switch from stocks to bonds, from gold shares to a money market fund, without paying costly commissions! The mutual fund families are adding new funds all the time. It's possible to make spectacular capital gains, or take advantage of high interest rates. Clearly, using mutual fund families is the easiest and least costly way to manage your pension funds.

INVESTMENT STRATEGIES IN YOUR PENSION PLAN

How should you invest your pension plan? What types of investments should you emphasize, and what kinds should be avoided?

First of all, consider your pension plan as a part of your overall estate planning. Besides your pension program, you have other sources of income and profit—your work, your investment portfolio, your home, and perhaps other retirement plans, such as social security. Your ultimate goal is *maximum profits* for your total estate at *minimum cost.*

Therefore, you must take into account the tax results of certain investment vehicles. For example, long-term capital gains are taxed as "ordinary income" when they are withdrawn from your pension, but they are 60% tax-free outside of your pension. Interest and dividends, on the other hand, are fully taxable as "ordinary income" whether in or outside of your pension fund.

The appropriate strategy would be to keep long-term capital gains outside your pension as much as possible; earn high interest and dividends inside your pension plan.

INVESTMENTS TO AVOID

Let us look at the investments you should avoid in your pension plan.

First, most long-term capital gains. Avoid such illiquid capital assets in your pension as coins, stamps, and other collectibles. These belong in your ordinary investment portfolio. This same principle applies to growth stocks that you plan to hold for longer than a year. You will lose the 60% tax-free advantage if you have them inside a pension. The one exception might be if you are the custodian of a corporate pension plan, and you want to buy a collectible that you never intend to sell. For example, you may want the joy of owning an original Picasso. You can deduct the cost of the painting by making it a part of your pension program. As custodian of the fund, you may decide to store the painting in your living room. Since you don't plan to sell it, it doesn't matter that you lose its capital gain status.

Second, investments that are already tax-sheltered. These include fixed and variable annuities, whole life insurance, All-Savers Certificates, tax-exempt bonds, and tax-free money market funds (those that invest in municipal bonds). There are no advantages at all to having double tax shelters. In fact, the costs are high. Yields on tax-exempt investments like municipal bonds and fixed annuities are lower, and there are additional administrative fees with variable annuities. Annuities and municipal bonds may make sense *outside* your pension plan and should have a place in your regular investment program. But they make no sense at all inside a tax-deferred retirement plan. Don't make the mistake of setting up a pension plan with an insurance company!

This advice also applies to Swiss franc annuities, a popular investment vehicle among older Americans. These are already tax-deferred and therefore don't belong in a self-directed pension plan. Swiss annuities are best for those who are about to reach retirement, or who have already retired. Then, of course, you can "roll over" your IRA or Keogh into a Swiss annuity when you wish to start withdrawing your retirement funds—but not until then.

A few investment advisers recommend real estate in your pension program. Again, income-producing property already has great tax advantages outside of a pension program. You would lose the value of depreciation and interest deductions if you put real estate into your retirement program.

Third, bank plans. Passbook accounts and certificates of deposit do not belong in your pension plan because the former do not pay enough interest and the latter are too illiquid. You can certainly gain a better return by investing with a brokerage house or mutual fund family. Banks that offer a totally self-directed plan with freedom to invest in any stock, bond, or mutual fund are fine, but don't tie up your funds in a limited bank program. These simply won't keep up with inflation in the long run.

RECOMMENDED INVESTMENTS

Now that you know what to avoid, what should you invest in? Consider the following possibilities:

First, high interest and dividends. Money market funds earn high interest (as high as 18% in 1981) and are very liquid. When interest rates peak, you can lock in those high yields by switching to bonds, corporate or government bond funds, or utilities. Then, when interest rates drop, you will not only continue to earn high yields, but will make capital gains as well. Once interest rates reach bottom, or start to climb again, sell the bonds and return to a money market fund or other investment vehicle. You can't "buy and hold" long-term bonds or utilities any more if you want to stay ahead of inflation.

Second, I also recommend holding some gold shares that pay high dividends. Some South African gold shares have been paying 20–30% annual yields! In addition, they offer the possibility of capital gains as inflation worsens. I do not recommend holding *non-dividend* gold shares in South Africa or North America in your pension plan. Remember, you want to stress high yields in your pension, not long-term capital gains. Also, while S.A. gold shares present a tempting opportunity for spectacular yields, be aware of the political risk and don't invest too heavily in South Africans.

Despite the 1981 tax law prohibiting collectibles in self-directed pension plans, you can still invest in gold, at least indirectly, through gold shares or gold mutual funds. The law does not apply to securities or mutual funds. I don't recommend gold coins in your pension anyway, but gold shares or gold funds that pay high dividends are worth considering during times of rapid inflation.

Third, short-term capital gains. You might consider trading or speculating in your self-directed retirement plan, to earn short-term capital gains (held for less than one year). The mutual fund families offer telephone-switching privileges that allow you to switch from one fund to another at any time without penalty, commissions, or tax consequences.

Technical trading systems that have been developed using no-load mutual funds typically result in *short-term* capital gains. Dick Fabian's system, which uses a 39-week moving average on all indices, has resulted in substantial short-term profits. If you are interested in using his method in your pension program you should get a copy of his book, *How to Be Your Own Investment Counselor—Through the Use of Telephone-Switch Mutual Funds* (Dick Fabian, Telephone-Switch Newsletter, P.O. Box 2538, Huntington Beach, CA 92647; $19.95). You'll receive the book free if you subscribe to his monthly newsletter, *Telephone-Switch Newsletter* ($97 a year). Highly recommended!

BE YOUR OWN MONEY MANAGER

Costs will be lowest if you are your own money manager, deciding for yourself when to change investment vehicles. You will undoubtedly make mistakes, but you will learn from those mistakes and your ability will improve. You don't learn anything by blindly turning your money over to an "expert" money manager. Several studies have shown that, on average, individual investors have better trading records than the so-called professionals!

By staying with money market funds, which will continue to pay high yields, you will not risk your principal, but I doubt that you will beat inflation over the long run. You must be willing to become an "informed speculator" if you wish to stay ahead and be financially independent when you reach retirement.

WHEN TO WITHDRAW YOUR RETIREMENT MONEY

Someday you will need to decide when to start withdrawing your money for retirement. The law discourages withdrawals from your Keogh or IRA before age 59½ by imposing a 10% penalty. But you must begin making withdrawals by age 70½.

Despite the 10% penalty, you should not simply forget about the money in your Keogh or IRA before age 59½. If a real emergency arises, or another important need comes up, you might consider withdrawing some of your money. Remember that the compounding of interest or dividends over a long period of time will produce dramatic results, so the penalty will not wipe out the interest you have accrued.

In addition, if you become disabled prior to age 59½, the penalty will be waived.

When you begin withdrawing your money, it will be subject to federal and state income taxes.

There are several ways to withdraw your money. You could take it out in a lump sum, but this might have severe tax consequences, probably putting you into the 50% tax bracket. The IRS allows Keogh participants to take advantage of a 10-year averaging rule, whereby you're taxed as if you had received the money over 10 years. But IRAs are limited to the normal 5-year income-averaging rule.

A more conservative approach would be to withdraw your money in equal installments. The total amount withdrawn for the year would be taxable as ordinary income.

Another possibility is to roll over your pension program into an annuity and receive a lifetime guaranteed monthly income, which is taxable as it is received. The only drawback to this idea is that U.S. annuities do not yet provide inflation protection once you annuitize. If you receive $1,000 a month when the annuity begins, you'll be getting $1,000 a month for the rest of your life—no less, and no more. In an era of high inflation, your purchasing power would be wiped out.

As an alternative, many retired Americans consider Swiss franc annuities, which offer built-in inflation protection for Americans. The pension plan is rolled over into a Swiss annuity, which pays a monthly check in Swiss francs. As the Swiss franc appreciates in value against the dollar, your monthly check is worth more. For example, if an American had purchased a Swiss annuity in 1970 that paid $1,000 a month, by 1982 he would be receiving over $2,500 a month! Now that's inflation protection. As long as the Swiss maintain a lower inflation rate than the United States, the franc will continue to appreciate against the dollar. For further information on Swiss annuities, write International Insurance Specialists, P.O.

Box 949, 1211 Geneva 3, Switzerland; or Assurex S. A., P.O. Box 290, 8033 Zurich, Switzerland.

The fourth possibility is to withdraw money as you need it, leaving any remainder to your beneficiaries, or to your children or relatives, when you die. You can bequeath your pension funds to your heirs or favorite tax-exempt organization (charity, church, college, etc.) without owing estate taxes.

Problem Solver #7

Q. I have a small professional corporation with a few employees. I have a pension/profit-sharing plan, but I can only contribute 25% of my salary. That still meant paying $25,000 in corporate income taxes last year. Is there any way I can cut it down to size?

A. Your situation is ideal for switching into a defined-benefit pension plan. Under this kind of corporate retirement plan, you can contribute up to 100% of your salary. How much you contribute depends on your age, cost of living in the future, and other criteria. You should definitely contact a corporate pension specialist. Corporate pension programs must include other employees, but since they earn a smaller salary, their contribution levels will be lower.

The end result is that your corporate tax liability will be cut to zero. You can also maintain total control over the money in your pension program, because you can be your own trustee.

9

—How to Form Your Own Tax-Exempt Organization

TAX-EXEMPT organizations have become so popular and so large that they may well be called the "third sector" of the U.S. economy, behind business and government. It is established that there are nearly a million organizations that fall under the category of public service, nonprofit, or charitable institutions. Annual revenues total $500 billion. These nonprofit organizations, which include churches, universities, hospitals, charities, associations, and foundations, own 11% of the property in the United States and employ 5% of the U.S. work force!

Tax-exempts are growing rapidly because of their unique tax and economic advantages. The IRS now processes 36,000 applications for tax-exempt status each year.

REASONS FOR STARTING YOUR OWN NONPROFIT ORGANIZATION

Why should you start your own tax-exempt organization or foundation? There are several significant reasons.

1. *Tax exemption.* Once tax-exempt status is approved by the IRS, the organization avoids federal taxes on all income. In addition, most states automatically approve tax-exempt status once the organization has achieved federal exemption, so state and local income

taxes are avoided as well. In most cases, this even includes local business fees and property taxes.

2. *Tax-free investment program.* Idle funds that have not been disbursed or spent can be invested by the organization in virtually any investment vehicle, including stocks and bonds, precious metals, collectibles, real estate, or money market funds. Any interest, dividends, or capital gains earned from these investment funds can accumulate completely tax-free. Since no taxes are paid on the earnings, the trustee can concentrate on maximum return and not worry about tax-sheltered investments, which often have lower returns. The head of a nonprofit organization would no longer be interested in investing in municipal bonds, annuities, or passbook savings accounts.

3. *Exemption from payroll taxes.* This is an extremely important advantage in today's world of high payroll taxes. Tax-exempt organizations have the *option* of participating in social security, and many have decided not to burden their employees with payment into the teetering fund. Even the director's salary is not subject to social security if the organization decides not to participate. In fact, the director has to sign a "waiver certificate" (Form SS-15) if he *does* want to be a part of social security; if the organization wishes not to participate, it needs to do nothing. Working for a nonparticipating organization does not jeopardize benefits for which a worker may already have qualifed in previous jobs, so this option can be extremely attractive.

An exempt organization does not have to pay federal unemployment compensation either. Most states still exempt such organizations from state unemployment compensation as well, but there are some exceptions; California is one. As unemployment rises in the United States, this unemployment tax often amounts to 1.5% or more of employees' salaries, so the savings can be significant.

4. *Avoiding state and local sales taxes.* When making purchases for the organization, a buyer simply presents a state tax-exempt number, and the sales tax will not be charged. In high-tax states, such as New York, this can be a substantial savings.

5. *Low postage rates.* The U.S. Postal Service allows nonprofit organizations to send mass mailings at a special third-class rate, which is currently 5.6 cents. This is substantially below the normal bulk rate of 10.4 cents, and the first-class cost of 20 cents. This is a spectacular discount, and can save thousands of dollars for organizations that do

a lot of mailing. There is an application fee to receive a permit number and an additional annual fee, but both fees are quite low.

6. *Generous deductions for contributors.* Most exempt organizations engage in fundraising. Contributions of up to 50% of a contributor's adjusted gross income can be deducted if the organization is a public charity or foundation, up to 20% if it is a private foundation. This gives potential contributors a great financial incentive to support the altruistic efforts of the organization.

The 50% deduction rule applies to the founder and director as well. You can contribute up to 50% of your adjusted gross income to your own public foundation, and take the deduction on your personal income tax return. There are some regulations governing how much a public foundation can accept from a single donor, however. This will be discussed shortly.

7. *Fringe benefits.* Tax-exempt organizations can operate as any other business does in terms of employee benefit programs. Your organization can offer life insurance, medical benefits, a pension program, etc., as discussed in other chapters of this book.

There are several other interesting benefits of a tax-exempt organization. For instance, it is not subject to collective-bargaining rules. Also, organizations with educational and charitable purposes can be exempt from U.S. Customs import duties.

THE GOALS OF YOUR ORGANIZATION

As you can see, the tax advantages of an exempt organization are tremendous. Fortunately, there are a surprising number of activities which, if set up properly, can qualify for tax-exempt status.

Generally the section of the U.S. Tax Code that qualifies such organizations is Section 501(c). The IRS divides qualified organizations into two parts: first, private foundations, and second, public charities.

Private Foundations

Private foundations are essentially grant-making institutions established by a wealthy individual or family. There are about 22,000 such foundations in the United States today. Those who established the private foundation are frequently the largest contributors. They can give up to 20% of their adjusted gross income in tax-deductible contributions. Typically a minimum endowment or investment fund of $500,000 is needed to start a grant-making program. Investment earnings are then used to finance annual grants for a variety of causes, from community services to scientific research.

The 1969 Tax Reform Act and other legislation have placed a number of restrictions on private foundations and their donors. In the past, wealthy individuals had established private foundations solely as a method of avoiding estate taxes and personally benefiting the founders and their relatives. The 1969 act imposed financial restrictions on "disqualified persons," or on individuals who might engage in "self-dealing," taking actions that would benefit them personally at the expense of the organization's goals. It also imposed federal excise taxes on the private foundation in certain circumstances. Needless to say, the 1969 act reduced the popularity of private foundations. Still, they can be a valuable tool for wealthy investors.

For more information on private foundations, I recommend you get a copy of "Why Establish a Private Foundation?" from the Council on Foundations, 1828 L Street, NW, Washington, DC 20006.

Public Charities

Public charities are broadly defined in section 501(c)(3) as follows:

1. *Charitable organizations* for:
   Relief of the poor or underprivileged
   Lessening the burdens of government (political action falls under this category, but lobbying efforts or actual support of political candidates is limited)
   Advancement of religion, education, or science
   Combating juvenile delinquency
   Defense of human and civil rights
   Establishment of a hospital, clinic, old-age home, or a public-interest law firm
   Establishment of fraternal organizations
   Bettering the conditions of labor, such as labor unions or employee associations

2. *Religious organizations:*
   Churches which conduct religious worship
   Missions, youth groups, and other auxiliaries
3. *Scientific organizations:*
   Aiding scientific education of a college or university
   Discovering a cure for disease
   Research in applied or natural sciences
   Publications of technical scientific information
4. *Educational organizations:*
   Instruction to the public on subjects beneficial to the public
     (must be fair presentation of all points of view, not simply
     propaganda or unsupported opinion)
   Establishment of a school or college consisting of a regularly
     scheduled curriculum, faculty, student body, etc.
   Public discussion groups on radio, TV, forums, etc.
   Publication of subjects of interest to the general public
   Museums, zoos, planetariums, symphony orchestras, etc.
5. *Organizations promoting amateur sports competition*
6. *Promotion of public safety*
7. *Prevention of cruelty to children and animals*

There are many other kinds of organizations that are eligible for tax exemption in other areas of the 501(c) section of the Tax Code, including federal credit unions, civic leagues, agricultural organizations, chambers of commerce, recreational clubs, teachers' retirement fund associations, benevolent life insurance associations, cemetery companies, pension trusts, veterans' organizations, black-lung benefit trusts, cooperatives, and political parties.

START YOUR OWN RELIGION?

The idea of starting your own church was popularized by "the Reverend" Kirby J. Hensley, founder of the Universal Life Church, a mail-order ministry that accepts virtually anyone's beliefs. After lengthy court battles with the IRS, the Universal Life Church was finally granted federal tax-exempt status in 1974, and it is now recognized in most states. Thus, by sending a $50 donation to the Universal Life Church, you can be ordained a minister and open branch services in your home or in any location. If you have a genuine congregation and hold regular services in your home or elsewhere, you can apply to the local county assessor for a religious exemption from real estate taxes.

You can also obtain a state tax-exempt number to avoid sales taxes, and a federal exempt number to avoid federal income taxes. In essence, a church is exempt from taxation, just as any other public charity is. An ordained minister does have to pay income taxes on his salary, but a "rental allowance" on his home (mortgage or rent, utilities, interest, and repair expenses) is considered tax-free income.

A minister can also take a once-in-a-lifetime exemption from social security, although the exemption does not apply to *non*religious income. To obtain this exemption, you must be recognized by the IRS as a duly ordained minister, legally authorized to perform marriages, funerals, and other ecclesiastical duties in your state.

You cannot, however, assign income from your nonreligious business or your secular job to your church to avoid federal and state income and employment taxes. This tax-avoidance ploy has been tried and defeated in the federal courts. *Unrelated business activity* is taxable, even for religious organizations. If a church operates a television or radio station for religious programming, it would be tax-exempt. But if it owned an office building for dentists, the rent would be taxable income. To take advantage of the religious exemption, you must be engaged in legitimate religious activities.

For details on starting your own church, get a copy of IRS Publication 517, "Tax Guide for Ministers and Religious Workers," and a minister's tax preparation guide from a local religious bookstore.

WHAT YOU CAN'T DO WITH AN EXEMPT ORGANIZATION

Now that you've seen how flexible a tax-free foundation can be, you should be aware of its limitations. Over the years, Congress has felt that some abuses have crept into these exempt organizations, and has thus imposed certain restrictions on them.

First, you cannot simply convert your current business into a tax-exempt organization. Your business must clearly fall under the categories listed earlier in this chapter to qualify as a "public charity." Unless you are a church, you have to apply formally to the IRS for exemption.

However, it is amazing how many corporations have been able to qualify. Recently, for instance, *Ms.* magazine revised its corporate status to become a tax-exempt organization. *Reason* magazine, a libertarian publication, followed the same basic approach to become a tax-free foundation. Other nonprofit organizations publish such magazines as *National Geographic* and *Smithsonian.* Lower mailing costs have made it possible for these magazines to keep their prices at a competitive level.

In 1950, a tax reform act was passed that taxed "unrelated business income" of exempt organizations. Under this ruling, a charitable foundation would be taxed on a business or trade that was not directly related to its exempt purposes. For example, a church that rented apartments would have to pay taxes on the rental income. The rules are not always clear, and sometimes public charities have to battle the IRS over what is "unrelated business" and what isn't. Questions arise, particularly if the unrelated business income is used for charitable activities.

Tax-exempt corporations or trusts are not allowed to declare dividends or profit-sharing among shareholders or directors. This would undoubtedly jeopardize their tax-exempt status. You must realize that once you establish a public organization, it is a separate legal entity—and you cannot get your money back after you've made donations, even if you're the director, except through reasonable salary payments.

The same principle applies to what the IRS calls "self dealing," or engaging in activities for the private benefits of directors or shareholders. There are many restrictions on the kinds of financial benefits that are available to major donors or creators of a private or public foundation. This does not mean, however, that you can't take a salary, or receive fringe benefits available to other employees of the organization. But you are required to report all such benefits and compensation in an annual IRS report (form 990).

The only other significant restriction applies to lobbying efforts and support of political candidates. Under current regulations, your foundation cannot use over 20% of its funds to promote activities attempting to influence specific legislation. Second, it cannot use a substantial portion (again, not more than 20%) in attempting to support or defeat a political candidate. Most financial experts in this field recommend that you avoid this kind of activity altogether in the beginning, when you are applying for tax-exempt status, because it may delay qualification.

You should also be careful not to be labeled a "political action" organization promoting just one point of view. Even though, from a practical point of view, this would be difficult for the IRS to prove, you want to avoid harassment from the government. The best kinds of political organizations are "educational" in nature, offering a variety of viewpoints, while emphasizing their own.

Finally, it's best that you involve the "public" in your tax-exempt foundation as much as possible. You want to encourage small donations from many contributors, not just a few large donations from wealthy individuals.

HOW TO GET STARTED

To set up your own tax-free foundation, you need to make several decisions.

First and foremost, you need to establish goals that will qualify for tax exemption under the headings of educational, religious, scientific, or charitable purposes.

Second, you should determine whether you wish to establish a public charity or a private foundation. As I've emphasized in this chapter, the public charity will be more useful in most cases.

Third, you need to determine the form of organization. There are basically two choices, a nonprofit corporation or a trust. A corporation usually has more requirements in terms of record keeping, government fees and paperwork, and additional regulations. A trust often provides greater flexibility. You can use either one. In either case, you should be aware that your organization's financial activities are made available to the public by the IRS. This applies to private as well as public foundations.

Fourth, you need to decide whether to establish the tax-exempt organization yourself, or to use an attorney.

DOING IT YOURSELF

It is possible to set up a nonprofit organization yourself for very little money. An acquaintance of mine recently started his own public educational foundation for less than $100. He began by obtaining a copy of IRS publication 557, "How to Apply for and Retain Exempt Status for Your Organization" (available at your local

IRS office). He then learned how to file for a nonprofit corporation by obtaining how-to information from his state's attorney general's office. His exempt status was approved in about two months. However, the IRS documents are fairly complex, and I think that this would be a difficult route to take unless you understand law very well.

Another "do-it-yourself" method is through Ted Nicholas' organization, the Company Corporation, which charges about $120 to set up a nonprofit organization for you in Delaware. Nicholas shows the advantage of using a tax-exempt organization in Delaware, which allows you to run the whole corporation alone if you wish. For information, I highly recommend Ted Nicholas' new book, *How to Form Your Own Non-Profit Corporation Without a Lawyer for Under $75.00* (Enterprise Publishing, Inc., 725 Market St., Wilmington, DE 19801; $14.95).

USING A LAWYER

Frankly, I think the best way to set up a tax-exempt foundation is through a tax attorney who has had experience with them. It's very important that you use someone who is experienced in this area, because certain specific language is required when filing with the IRS. Another advantage is that a tax-exempt specialist will have streamlined the whole filing process so that your costs and waiting time will be lower. A good lawyer will charge anywhere from $1,500 and up to set up a trust-type foundation. Corporate foundations often cost more.

A tax-exempt specialist will discuss all the options with you, and offer suggestions as to goals, contributions, and regulations. I am familiar with several attorneys who have established a number of trusts, but publishing their names would probably overwhelm them. I recommend that you search for competent legal counsel in your own area before you attempt to use someone in a distant city.

Your attorney will assist you in filing IRS Form 1023, "Application for Recognition of Exemption Under Section 501(c)(3) of the Internal Revenue Code." After you list the goals you wish to achieve through your organization, he will restate those goals in the precise language necessary to obtain quick approval from the IRS.

Approval can take anywhere from two to six months. This will only be an "advance ruling," since you have not been in business yet, and therefore have not established a business history. This advance ruling lasts for two to three years. If, during these initial years, the IRS is satisfied that your organization operates properly under Section 501(c) statutes, it will issue a "definitive" or final ruling.

HOW TO SET UP YOUR OWN FOUNDATION WITHOUT FILING

It is actually possible to enjoy the advantages of a foundation without ever filing with the IRS, or paying the expenses of a tax attorney. This is accomplished by setting up a "donor account" inside a national foundation that has already been IRS-approved. Very few foundations have this capability, but you may wish to investigate the ones that do.

For example, National Heritage Foundation, in Annandale, Va., is a broadly based "public charitable trust" that permits you to operate under its banner with your own account number. You make tax-deductible contributions directly to the foundation, and then request that your funds be used according to your desires. Of course, you can only recommend activities that would fall under the broad categories permitted under Section 501(c)(3), i.e., religious, educational, scientific, or charitable activities. The National Heritage Foundation, in turn, keeps the books and the payroll accounts, issues all checks, receives all contributions, and files all reports to the federal and state authorities. They are audited every year—at their request!—in order to make sure everything is run properly.

The biggest drawback, besides the bureaucratic problems associated with going through another organization, is that National Heritage Foundation charges an 8½% fee on all contributions made to your account, a sizable amount. Frankly, unless you really despise paperwork, you would probably save more money setting up your own foundation.

There are other large foundations that accept "donor accounts" for little or no fees if they approve of your activities. Naturally, they don't want the publicity, but you can call around locally to see if any exist in your area.

WILL YOU BE AUDITED?

Your tax-exempt organization is subject to audit, just as any other corporation or taxpayer is. Even though you may owe no tax, you still must file annual tax returns (form 990). Form 990-T is used if you have unrelated business activity, which is taxable if earnings are more than $1,000.

With nearly a million tax-exempt organizations, the IRS relies heavily on analyzing the 990 information returns rather than physically auditing the organization. It does have specialists who audit tax-exempts, and there seems to be a tendency to audit organizations that appear to have engaged in "political action," propaganda activities, or discriminatory practices that might eliminate their tax-exempt status. But if you maintain a low profile and stay within the general guidelines, your chances of a full-scale audit are slim.

HOW TO KEEP UP TO DATE

Having a tax-exempt public foundation will require careful planning and administration. I recommend that you keep up to date on the latest changes in the tax laws, IRS rulings, court decisions, etc., by subscribing to *Tax Exempt News* (Capitol Publications, Inc., 1300 North 17th Street, Arlington, VA 22209; $87 for 12 monthly issues).

In addition, some of the "big eight" accounting firms offer free publications on the management and accounting of tax-exempts and have departments that specialize in this area.

Problem Solver #8

Q. We run a very successful private school in our home town. It's so successful that we paid $30,000 in payroll taxes last year, and are starting to pay income taxes on our profits. What can we do to reduce this tax burden? We could sure use the money for more worthwhile expansion!

A. Consider switching the legal status of your school to a nonprofit educational institution. This may mean greater scrutiny by the IRS, to make sure it's "nondiscriminatory," but it may be worth the tax savings. By becoming non-profit, you and your teachers no longer have to participate in social security. If you drop out of social security, it may be a good idea to substitute your own retirement program. It should be fairly easy to show your teachers that they can contribute less and get more out of their own retirement program than they would if they stayed with social security. In addition, a nonprofit organization can accumulate profits completely tax-free, and use the money for expansion, investments, etc. Finally, by being a nonprofit school, you can take *tax-deductible* contributions from the children's parents and other school supporters.

10

—The State Tax Havens

WHILE MANY international investors have considered the advantages of offshore tax havens, many investors may be unaware of the tremendous tax savings available right here in the United States. There are, for example, five states that do not impose a general sales tax, seven states that do not have an income tax, four states that do not tax corporate income, and one state that has no death or gift taxes.

You and your business can save thousands of dollars by carefully selecting the state in which you live. On average, state and local taxes have increased much faster than federal taxation. As local taxes reach sky-high levels, more and more taxpayers are considering moving to another state as a way to reduce their tax liabilities. While taxation should never be the only reason for moving, it can be a very important consideration.

While some states may not impose certain kinds of taxes, they often make up the deficit by imposing above-average rates in other areas. For example, New Hampshire has no income tax, but property taxes are among the highest in the nation. On the other hand, California has a high income tax, but a very low property tax now, thanks to Proposition 13. Who would fare better in terms of tax savings—a New Hampshire resident or a California resident? Through a little financial planning, a California resident could reduce or eliminate his state income tax liabilities, while paying very little in property taxes. The New Hampshire resident has only two options available to him, either purchase a less valuable home or rent a place. He will have an extremely difficult time reducing his property taxes if he owns a home.

Thus, it is very important to look at what kinds of taxes are imposed in each state, and then to look at the overall tax burden on a per capita and income basis. The maps and tables in this chapter, prepared by the Tax Foundation, Inc., show how each state ranks in terms of overall taxation. Some of the figures may be deceptive, however. For example, Alaska's per capita tax is very high, but most of its revenue comes from tax on oil production, not on individuals directly. Since Alaska has few residents but lots of oil, the per capita tax appears high.

In reviewing individual states, we will take a look at the most significant kinds of taxation, on income, sales, property, inheritance, etc.

HOW TO AVOID STATE INCOME TAXES

State taxes on individual income vary considerably—from none at all in Alaska, Florida, Nevada, South Dakota, Texas, Washington, and Wyoming, to a high in Minnesota of 16%! The most expensive locations are California, Delaware, Hawaii, Iowa, Maine, Minnesota, Montana, New York, Oregon, Wisconsin, and the District of Columbia, which all have rates of 10% or more on high-income residents.

But a state's high income tax should not necessarily deter you from living there. By engaging in high-deduction shelters, you can reduce your state income tax liabilities to almost any level. Some investors in high-tax states are attracted to Treasury bills, notes, and bonds, for example, because they are not subject to state or local income taxes.

Since so much revenue comes from income taxes, there is admittedly a greater possibility that state treasury agents will audit your return. This is particularly true if you are in a high tax bracket or if you show a large number of deductions. This higher audit potential is one reason that many private investors would prefer living in one of the seven states listed above where they do not even have to file a state tax return.

HOW TO AVOID STATE AND LOCAL SALES TAXES

Like state income taxes, sales tax rates vary from state to state, and even from city to city. Four states have no sales levy at all—Delaware, Montana, New Hampshire, and Oregon. Alaska imposes no

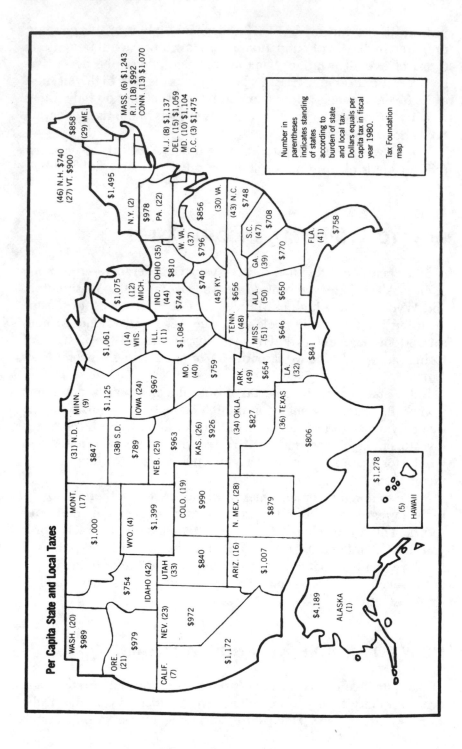

Per Capita State and Local Taxes

Number in parentheses indicates standing of states according to burden of state and local tax. Dollars equals per capita tax in fiscal year 1980.

Tax Foundation map

MASS. (6) $1,243
R.I. (18) $992
CONN. (13) $1,070

N.J. (8) $1,137
DEL. (15) $1,059
MD. (10) $1,104
D.C. (3) $1,475

(46) N.H. $740
(27) VT. $900
(29) ME. $858

N.Y. (2) $1,495
PA. (22) $978

W. VA. (37) $796
VA. (30) $856
N.C. (43) $748
S.C. (47) $708
GA. (39) $770
FLA. (41) $758

OHIO (35) $810
KY. (45) $740
TENN. (48) $656
ALA. (50) $650
MISS. (51) $646
LA. (32) $841

IND. (44) $744
ILL. (11) $1,084
MICH. (12) $1,075
WIS. (14) $1,061

ARK. (49) $654
MO. (40) $759
IOWA (24) $967
MINN. (9) $1,125

OKLA. (34) $827
TEXAS (36) $806
KAS. (26) $926
NEB. (25) $963
S.D. (38) $789
N.D. (31) $847

COLO. (19) $990
N. MEX. (28) $879
WYO. (4) $1,399
MONT. (17) $1,000

ARIZ. (16) $1,007
UTAH (33) $840
IDAHO (42) $754

NEV. (23) $972
ORE. (21) $979
WASH. (20) $989

CALIF. (7) $1,172

ALASKA (1) $4,189

HAWAII (5) $1,278

State-Local Taxes by State[a]
Per Capita and Per $1,000 of Personal Income
Fiscal Years 1970 and 1980

State	Per capita taxes				Taxes per $1,000 of personal income			
	Amount		Percent increase	Rank 1980	Amount		Percent change	Rank 1980
	1970	1980			1970	1980		
U.S. AVERAGE	$427	$ 987	131	—	$117	$116	− 1	—
Alabama	259	650	151	50	98	96	− 1	46
Alaska	417	4,189	904	1	100	368	267	1
Arizona.............	425	1,007	137	16	132	133	(b)	7
Arkansas	252	654	160	49	98	99	1	43
California	559	1,172	110	7	134	122	− 9	15
Colorado	419	990	136	19	122	113	− 7	24
Connecticut	485	1,070	121	13	107	105	− 1	35
Delaware	450	1,059	135	15	111	116	4	19
Florida	347	758	118	41	105	97	− 7	45
Georgia	312	770	147	39	100	108	7	31
Hawaii	572	1,278	123	5	144	148	2	4
Idaho	347	754	117	42	117	104	−11	38
Illinois	487	1,084	123	11	114	112	− 2	25
Indiana	357	744	108	44	98	88	−10	51
Iowa	436	967	122	24	125	111	−11	27
Kansas	395	926	135	26	110	100	− 9	42
Kentucky	299	740	147	45	105	104	− 1	37
Louisiana	331	841	154	32	116	116	(b)	20
Maine	380	858	126	29	126	125	− 1	11
Maryland	482	1,104	129	10	123	120	− 2	16
Massachusetts	497	1,243	150	6	124	139	12	5
Michigan	456	1,075	136	12	115	115	(b)	22
Minnesota	442	1,125	154	9	125	127	2	9
Mississippi..........	296	646	119	51	125	109	−13	30
Missouri.............	343	759	122	40	100	93	− 7	49
Montana	398	1,000	151	17	127	130	2	8
Nebraska	396	963	143	25	112	111	− 2	28
Nevada	517	972	88	23	124	105	−15	36
New Hampshire	333	740	122	46	99	92	− 7	50
New Jersey	447	1,137	154	8	106	117	11	18
New Mexico	359	879	145	28	127	122	− 4	14
New York	652	1,495	129	2	146	163	12	2
North Carolina	311	748	141	43	105	106	1	33
North Dakota	376	847	125	31	125	102	−18	40
Ohio	343	810	136	35	91	94	3	48
Oklahoma	306	827	170	34	100	102	2	41
Oregon	400	979	145	21	115	114	− 1	23
Pennsylvania	401	978	144	22	110	116	5	21
Rhode Island........	408	992	143	18	110	119	8	17
South Carolina	274	708	158	47	101	107	5	32
South Dakota	398	789	98	38	133	106	−20	34
Tennessee	279	656	135	48	98	94	− 4	47
Texas...............	316	806	155	36	97	98	(b)	44
Utah	375	840	124	33	127	125	− 2	13
Vermont.............	471	900	91	27	147	127	−13	10
Virginia.............	340	856	151	30	102	102	(b)	39
Washington	443	989	123	20	115	109	− 6	29
West Virginia	301	796	164	37	111	112	1	26
Wisconsin	509	1,061	109	14	146	125	−15	12
Wyoming	434	1,399	223	4	134	148	10	3
District of Columbia ..	517	1,475	185	3	104	136	31	6

[a]Excludes unemployment compensation taxes.
[b]Less than .5%.
Source: Bureau of the Census, U.S. Department of Commerce; and Tax Foundation computations.

state sales tax, but it does have local sales taxes in some cities. North Dakota, Vermont, and West Virginia charge only 3%, statewide. But Connecticut charges 7.5%, Pennsylvania and the District of Columbia 6%, and New York City charges the highest in the country, 8%. Half the states exclude food purchases from taxation.

There are ways to avoid the sales tax, however, even if you live in a state that imposes one.

Nearly everyone has purchased something by mail from *out-of-state* companies, without even realizing that they were avoiding the sales tax. In most cases, an out-of-state purchase is free of state or local taxes. A wide variety of products can be bought through the mail—from prime cuts of meat and fresh fruits to household items and clothing to gold and silver coins—all without paying sales tax. The savings can be significant on high-priced items.

Some states have sought aggressively to reduce this out-of-state exemption. Years ago automobile purchases represented the greatest potential savings from buying out of state, as much as $200–$300 on a single purchase. Most states closed this loophole by imposing a registration fee, usually equal to the sales tax, when a car is brought into the state.

Today, most states have closed the mail-order loophole even further by requiring out-of-state companies to collect sales tax if they have an office or "business presence" (salesmen, delivery, or catalog pick-up service) in the state. Thus, Sears, Penney's, and other catalog stores will require sales tax, even though the order is fulfilled from out of state. Most specialty firms do not fit the "business presence" description, but it is becoming more frequent for large mail-order firms, such as Day-Timers, which sells office stationery, and the Franklin Mint, which sells commemorative medallions, to collect the sales tax.

Within states that have sales taxes, there are still some exemptions. Dealer-to-dealer, wholesale transactions are exempt from sales or use tax. Dealers receive a "tax-exempt number" from the state to use for business purchases.

Coin investors often take advantage of this dealer-to-dealer exemption by attending coin shows, which are held every few months in major cities. Dealers at most coin shows presume all customers to be fellow coin dealers, and therefore do not collect a sales tax.

Some states may have specific sales tax exemptions on certain investments. For instance, California imposes no sales tax on purchases of coins valued at over $1,000.

MINIMIZING LOCAL PROPERTY TAXES

All states in the union have local property taxes, but these levies differ considerably. According to the Tax Foundation, the states with the lowest property taxes are Alabama, Louisiana, Arkansas, Kentucky, West Virginia, New Mexico, and Mississippi, all in the southern U.S. The highest rates are in Alaska, Massachusetts, Wyoming, New Jersey, New York, and Connecticut. See the map and table for rates in your state.

California made a dramatic change in its property taxes following the passage of Proposition 13 in 1977. This reduced property levies to 1% of their assessed value. Even more important, the initiative limits the *increases* in property taxes to 2% a year. This fact will make California real estate more and more attractive in an inflationary environment, especially for long-term homeowners. Many politicians and armchair economists predicted massive unemployment and reduced services as a result of the lower tax, but just the opposite has come true. New jobs in the private sector have caused California's economy to boom.

WHICH STATE TAX HAVENS ARE BEST?

Let me highlight the tax advantages of a few low-tax states.

Texas

Oil is only one reason why Dallas, Houston, and other Texas cities are booming. Another reason is that Texas offers outstanding tax incentives to new businesses and individual investors. The Tax Foundation ranks Texas as the fifth-lowest state in terms of state and local taxes. Real estate is also relatively low-priced, except in certain wealthy areas in Houston and Dallas. Austin, the capital city, is among the nation's top 20 small metropolitan cities, with extremely attractive real estate prices.

Foremost among Texas' advantages is that it has no individual or corporate income tax. This not only saves you a great deal of money, but it preserves your privacy, because you do not have to give the state any financial information. Counties and cities in other states that have an income or business tax get copies of your state

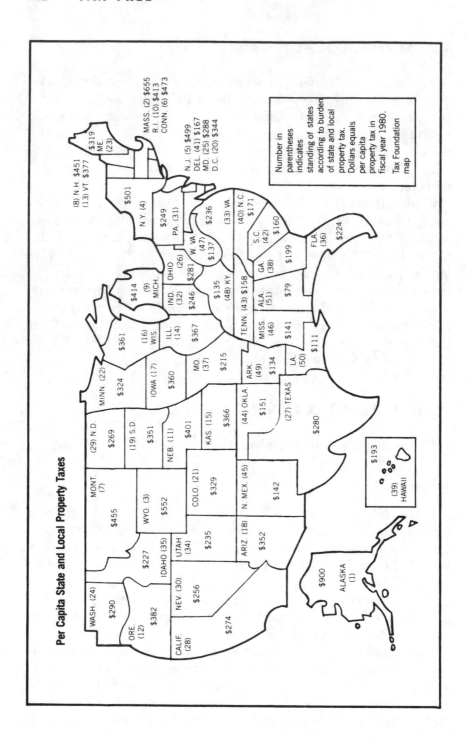

Per Capita State and Local Property Taxes

Number in parentheses indicates standing of states according to burden of state and local property tax. Dollars equals per capita property tax in fiscal year 1980.

Tax Foundation map

WASH. (24) $290
ORE. (12) $382
CALIF. (28) $274
NEV. (30) $256
IDAHO (35) $227
UTAH (34) $235
ARIZ. (18) $352
MONT. (7) $455
WYO. (3) $552
COLO. (21) $329
N. MEX. (45) $142
(29) N.D. $269
(19) S.D. $351
NEB. (11) $401
KAS. (15) $366
OKLA. (44) $151
TEXAS (27) $280
MINN. (22) $324
IOWA (17) $360
MO. (37) $367
ARK. (49) $134
LA. (50) $111
WIS. (16) $361
ILL. (14) $215
MICH. (9) $414
IND. (32) $246
OHIO (26) $281
KY. (48) $135
TENN. (43) $158
MISS. (46) $141
ALA. (51) $79
GA. (38) $199
FLA. (36) $224
W. VA (47) $137
VA. (33) $236
N.C. (40) $171
S.C. (42) $160
N.Y. (4) $501
PA. (31) $249
(8) N.H. $451
(13) VT. $377
ME. (23) $319
MASS. (2) $655
R.I. (10) $413
CONN. (6) $473
N.J. (5) $499
DEL. (41) $167
MD. (25) $288
D.C. (20) $344
HAWAII (39) $193
ALASKA (1) $900

Property Tax Collections by State
Per Capita and Per $1,000 of Personal Income
Fiscal Years 1970 and 1980

State	Per capita property tax				Property taxes per $1,000 of personal income			
	Amount		Percent increase	Rank 1980	Amount		Percent change	Rank 1980
	1970	1980			1970	1980		
TOTAL	$168	$302	80	—	$46	$35	− 22	—
Alabama	39	79	100	51	15	12	− 21	51
Alaska	102	900	785	1	24	79	223	1
Arizona	166	352	112	18	51	46	− 10	13
Arkansas	65	134	106	49	25	20	− 20	44
California	262	274	4	28	63	28	− 55	34
Colorado	179	329	84	21	52	38	− 28	21
Connecticut	238	473	98	6	52	47	− 11	11
Delaware	84	167	100	41	21	18	− 11	49
Florida	118	224	90	36	36	29	− 19	33
Georgia	95	199	109	38	31	28	− 9	36
Hawaii	98	193	96	39	25	22	− 10	43
Idaho	127	227	79	35	43	31	− 27	30
Illinois	201	367	83	14	47	38	− 19	20
Indiana	168	246	46	32	46	29	− 37	32
Iowa	213	360	69	17	61	41	− 32	18
Kansas	202	366	81	15	56	39	− 30	19
Kentucky	69	135	97	48	24	19	− 21	47
Louisiana	65	111	70	50	23	15	− 33	50
Maine	174	319	84	23	58	47	− 19	12
Maryland	156	288	84	25	40	31	− 21	29
Massachusetts	250	555	122	2	63	62	− 1	2
Michigan	184	414	125	9	47	44	− 5	16
Minnesota	171	324	90	22	48	37	− 24	22
Mississippi.............	71	141	97	46	30	24	− 22	41
Missouri	137	215	57	37	40	26	− 34	38
Montana	216	455	111	7	69	59	− 14	3
Nebraska	209	401	92	11	59	46	− 22	14
Nevada	178	256	44	30	43	28	− 35	37
New Hampshire	207	451	117	8	61	56	− 9	5
New Jersey	242	499	106	5	57	51	− 10	8
New Mexico	81	142	75	45	29	20	− 31	45
New York..............	237	501	111	4	53	55	3	6
North Carolina	79	171	117	40	27	24	− 9	39
North Dakota	175	269	54	29	58	32	− 41	25
Ohio	162	281	73	26	43	32	− 25	26
Oklahoma	93	151	63	44	30	19	− 39	48
Oregon	189	382	102	12	54	45	− 18	15
Pennsylvania	119	249	110	31	32	29	− 9	31
Rhode Island	165	413	150	10	45	50	11	9
South Carolina	61	160	160	42	23	24	6	40
South Dakota	219	351	60	19	73	47	− 36	10
Tennessee	77	158	105	43	27	22	− 17	42
Texas..................	128	280	118	27	39	34	− 14	24
Utah	135	235	74	34	46	35	− 24	23
Vermont...............	164	377	130	13	51	53	4	7
Virginia................	96	236	145	33	29	28	− 2	35
Washington	155	290	87	24	40	32	− 21	27
West Virginia	70	137	95	47	26	19	− 26	46
Wisconsin	220	361	64	16	63	42	− 33	17
Wyoming	206	552	168	3	64	58	− 9	4
District of Columbia	169	344	104	20	34	32	− 7	28

Source: Bureau of the Census, U.S. Department of Commerce; and Tax Foundation computations.

tax return, and tax you at the local level. Local governments won't learn about your income level and other financial data, either, because there are no county taxes other than the property tax. Also, investors will find it a lot simpler not to have to worry about state income taxes when buying municipal bonds.

Texas relies on several other sources for revenue. It has a sales tax of 4%, plus 1% at the county level. Property taxes are slightly lower than the national average. Texas gets a sizable portion of its revenue from an oil levy that is imposed at the well on Texas oil fields. Yet, even with this oil levy, Texas gasoline prices are about the cheapest in the country!

Nevada

Nevada, the "silver state" (also known as the gambling state), has some unique advantages. It has no state income tax, no corporate income tax, and no inheritance tax, and it is considered a low-cost, convenient place to set up a corporation. Chief revenues come from gambling fees, a 5.75% sales tax that excludes food and drugs, and local property taxes. Property taxes are moderately high, however. Las Vegas, Reno, and Carson City are the principal cities, and Lake Tahoe is fast becoming a resort and retirement haven for the rich. This mountain resort has top entertainment, gaming, and water and snow skiing. Needless to say, real estate prices are exorbitant in Tahoe.

Washington

Parts of Washington offer a unique situation. Its only technical tax advantage is that it does not have an individual or corporate income tax. In all other respects, its tax burden is around the national average (ranked 24th by the Tax Foundation).

But Washington shares a border with Oregon, which has no sales tax. This creates an unusual tax-savings opportunity for Washington residents who are living next to the Oregon border, particularly in the city of Vancouver, which is just across the Columbia River from Portland. By purchasing appliances, equipment, tools, and other major items in Oregon, Washingtonians can avoid the 5% sales tax imposed by their state. This can add up to a substantial savings over the years. This technique may even be worthwhile for upper-state residents of Seattle or Spokane when purchasing high-priced items.

New Hampshire

New Hampshire is the only state in the union that has neither a sales tax nor an individual income tax. It has no inheritance tax on spouses or legal heirs. It does, however, have an 8% tax on corporate income.

In addition, it imposes a 5% tax on any stock dividends you may earn, and on interest from local bank accounts as well.

The main source of revenue for the state is property taxes, making New Hampshire fifth-highest in the nation! This is virtually impossible for homeowners to avoid. Nevertheless, the Tax Foundation ranks New Hampshire one of the lowest-taxing states in the country, overall.

New Hampshire has become a popular tax haven for New Englanders, especially for people employed in nearby Boston. Massachusetts is notorious as a high-tax region. Property taxes are even higher there than in New Hampshire! In personal income terms Massachusetts is ranked the fourth-highest-tax state in the union. Workers employed in Boston cannot avoid Massachusetts income taxes by living in New Hampshire, however, because Massachusetts taxes both residents and workers. Many Massachusetts residents avoid their state's 5% sales tax by shopping in New Hampshire for high-ticket items.

Florida

Florida is a popular retirement area that has a relatively low tax base. It has no personal property tax and no individual income tax, which is a great benefit to the large retirement community that relies mostly on fixed incomes. It does, however, have a corporate income tax, and a 4% sales tax, except on food and drugs.

Alaska

It might seem strange to list Alaska as a state tax haven, considering that the Tax Foundation lists it as the state with the highest tax burden in the country! But because of higher oil and gas revenues, the "last frontier" state was able to abolish its personal income tax in 1980. Its government also recently withdrew its employees from the social security system.

Alaska also has no state sales tax, but some local boroughs and cities do impose sales taxes of 1–5%. Anchorage, the largest city, has no sales tax. Property taxes are high, though not as high as some statistics indicate. The Tax Foundation ranks Alaska as having the highest per capita property levies in the country, at $2,500 per resident. However, this figure is inflated by the property and severance tax Alaska imposes on oil and gas lands. Taxes on local residential property are more reasonable.

Alaska is known for its high salaries, as well as for its high cost of living. In sum, the decision to move to Alaska must depend on your personal situation. The culture, the weather, the distance—all are just as important as the financial structure of a state.

Wyoming and South Dakota

Wyoming and South Dakota are similar: They have no state income tax, a low sales tax, and low population. South Dakota recently reduced its state sales tax to 4%; Wyoming's sales tax is only 3%. Both states have a local sales tax of 1%.

SHOULD YOU MOVE TO A STATE TAX HAVEN?

Moving to a state that will significantly reduce your local taxes has to be weighed against other important goals. There may be numerous social, cultural, and financial reasons why you may not want to move. Not many people can enjoy the luxury of living anywhere they please.

Nevertheless, if you're searching for a new job or a place to retire, or particularly if you want to relocate your company, take a close look at the state tax havens—they may mean the difference between comfortable living and a real financial struggle.

Problem Solver #9

Q. I live in a state that is known as a "nuisance tax state." My business is doing pretty well, but I am hit with a new tax or more paperwork practically every week. If it isn't the state sales tax, it's a corporate income tax, or a gross receipts tax, or a personal property tax, or an unemployment compensation tax. Is there any way out of this mess, short of going on welfare?

A. Move to Texas! Texas is booming for the simple reason that it doesn't have all these "nuisance" taxes. There is no state or local income tax. No corporate income tax. No paperwork and red-tape bureaucracy. You'll save thousands of dollars, more than enough to pay for moving costs. And the Tax Foundation ranks Texas as the fifth-best state in the union for low taxes.

If you don't like Texas, check out Nevada, Florida, or some of the other popular low-tax states mentioned in this chapter.

11

—How to Avoid Estate Taxes

JOHN AND MARY were married for 40 years. They worked side by side in a family printing business, struggling in the early years but gradually increasing in prosperity until finally, by the time they were ready to retire, they had amassed an estate of nearly $1 million. Always an independent businessman, John had not taken advantage of estate-planning techniques. Then one day a few years ago Mary found herself printing John's memorial program; John had died.

Financially, Mary was not concerned. She still had the family business to support herself, as well as their savings and investments. But Mary was in for a shock.

The business she thought was hers now belonged to the taxable estate of her dead husband. Funds were tied up until probate, making it difficult for her to pay bills, payroll checks, and other business expenses. At probate she found that she owed nearly $150,000 in estate taxes. Since most of the estate's net worth was tied up in printing equipment and real estate, she had to cash all of her liquid investments to pay the bill. Then she received her lawyer's invoice—another $5,000. Six months earlier, John and Mary were on easy street; now, the business was floundering in desperate need of cash and Mary's retirement income was exhausted. In desperation she sold the business she had worked 40 years to build, and spent the rest of her life bitterly wishing John had planned ahead—or at least that he hadn't gone first. . . .

It was stories like this that brought about the new federal estate

148

tax law. The Economic Recovery Tax Act of 1981 made revolutionary changes in estate planning. Over the course of four years, it substantially increases the exemption level on federal estate taxes, so that eventually only large estates will incur a federal tax at the time of death. Even on those large estates, the maximum tax rate is reduced to 50%. Moreover, the new law allows a person to leave all property and valuables to the surviving spouse without paying any estate taxes at all.

In this chapter, we will examine specific ways to be completely exempt from state as well as federal estate taxes. The new law provides quite a few new wrinkles, and at times the techniques are quite complex. But reaching the ultimate goal of avoiding estate taxes is quite possible, if not probable, for all investors who take advantage of these exemptions.

THE NEW EXEMPTIONS

Under the new regulations, by 1987 an estate can completely avoid federal taxes on assets worth up to $600,000. Undoubtedly the law will be altered again to allow for continued inflation. The exemption schedule follows:

Year	Amount Not Subject to Federal Estate Tax	Lowest Tax Bracket Rate
1982	$225,000	32%
1983	$275,000	34%
1984	$325,000	34%
1985	$400,000	34%
1986	$500,000	37%
1987 and beyond	$600,000	37%

This is a substantial increase in the exemption level, considering that it stood at $175,000 in 1981. By 1987, the federal estate tax burden will be virtually eliminated for most Americans. And, by using several additional simple techniques, it's possible to have $1.2 million exempt!

MAXIMUM TAX RATES

While exemptions are going up, tax rates are coming down. The top rates for federal estate and gift taxes are reduced gradually to 50% by 1985. The following schedule applies:

Year	Top-Bracket Rate	Maximum Amount in Excess of:
1982	65%	$4.0 million
1983	60%	$3.5 million
1984	55%	$3.0 million
1985 and after	50%	$2.5 million

We can see from the above chart that the maximum rate is gradually reduced, but unfortunately the tax brackets are moving lower also. This means that the maximum rate applies at *lower* estate levels, demonstrating the real need to continue estate planning to avoid taxes at death. These figures may seem high when compared to your personal estate, but if inflation continues in this country and around the world, even these will be out of date sometime in the near future.

TAKING ADVANTAGE OF THE "UNLIMITED MARITAL DEDUCTION"

Under the new law, anything you leave your spouse will reduce the size of your estate, and you won't have to pay federal estate taxes on it. This is a dramatic departure from previous law, which limited the marital deduction to $250,000.

Many investors are rewriting their wills to reflect this important change. But let me offer *a word of caution.* Don't be too hasty in conferring all your property and valuables on your spouse, particularly if you have children who will eventually inherit the estate of both parents. Suppose, for example, that you and your spouse have combined assets of $1 million. You die, leaving everything to your spouse. No tax is owed on your estate because of the marital exclusion. One year later your spouse dies, leaving everything to the children. Since only $600,000 is exempt on nonmarital inheritances, the estate must now pay about $135,000 to the federal government!

A much better approach would have been to have divided your estate into two parts, so that each of you could have taken advantage of the full federal exemption. If both estates are settled after 1986, the combined estate could be valued at $1.2 million without either partner incurring federal estate taxes, assuming each had $600,000 in separate estates!

WHAT IF THE SURVIVING SPOUSE REMARRIES?

There has always been the concern that the surviving spouse may remarry and then leave everything to the new spouse, thereby depriving your heirs of an inheritance. The new law allows you to avoid this problem. Simply stipulate in your will that a particular piece of property or asset (stocks, bonds, real estate, gold, etc.) must be passed on to your children, or anyone else you name, after your spouse dies. In legal terms, this is called a "qualifying terminable interest property." It allows your spouse full use of the asset while living, but lets you decide who gets it after your spouse dies.

FEDERAL VERSUS STATE TAXES

There are numerous new rules that must be considered when preparing your will and dividing your estate so as to minimize *federal* estate taxes. Moreover, you should also take a close look at your *state* inheritance or estate laws. Undoubtedly each of the 50 states will be reexamining its estate taxes to conform with the new federal statutes, but it may take some time. It's quite possible that some states will continue to impose estate taxes at low levels to recoup losses from federal budget cuts. Fortunately, a dozen states exempt estates using the maximum federal credit, so they already conform to the new estate tax exclusions. But many states also impose *inheritance* taxes to be paid by the heirs, so you must be familiar with local death taxes when you engage in complete estate planning. If you have a sizable estate, you should have a local attorney help you set up your will.

KEEPING ASSETS OUT OF YOUR ESTATE

One of the principal objectives in your estate planning will be the least-costly transfer of valuables, property, and investments from your estate to your heirs, favorite charities, or other recipients, and perhaps to your own personal public foundation.

Estate planning should be done as early as possible. Your options are severely limited if you wait until you're on your deathbed. The more valuable your property or assets are, the more difficult it will be to transfer them out of your estate *without* tax consequences.

Transferring Company Stock to Heirs

Suppose you are president of a small manufacturing company that has a great future—perhaps it will soon be a leading growth company in its field. You wisely decide to divide your company stock into two types, preferred stock and common stock. The *preferred stock* gets preference over common stock, in the sense that if the company does not earn enough to pay a dividend to both classes of stock, only the preferred stockholders will be paid. The preferred stock pays a modest rate of return but has a low value. The common stock produces less income, but has greater growth potential. As president of the company, you elect to receive only preferred stock in the company, making sure that only preferred stockholders (yourself) will have complete control over the company.

The common stock reflects the growth in the company, and therefore should increase substantially in value over the years. As an estate tool, therefore, you give the common stock to your children at a time when the price is very low. When the company becomes a million-dollar firm, you have nicely transferred a major value of your estate to your heirs without paying estate or gift taxes.

This is the technique that was used by Dr. Joseph E. Salsbury with his pharmaceutical company, Salsbury Laboratories. At his death, the IRS valued his company at $13 million. However, due to a stock division years earlier, Dr. Salsbury's personal estate was assessed by the tax court at $514,000. Thus, he was able to transfer $12.5 million to his heirs without paying a penny in federal estate or gift taxes!

Suppose, on the other hand, that he had waited to divide the stock until the company had become a great success, and the company stock had already become extremely valuable. Dividing the company stock into preferred and common shares now, and transferring the common shares to his heirs, would only have resulted in hefty gift taxes, which are taxed at the same rate as estate taxes. Thus, we see the clear advantage of acting early when it comes to estate planning.

Stock recapitalization, as this is called, is a great idea for anyone in a closely held corporation.

Selling Your Property Using Long-Term Notes

Another shrewd technique for transferring your estate before death uses inflation to beat the revenue man. This is done by selling your valuables or property to your heirs, using a long-term installment note. The 1981 tax act eliminated the tricky installment sale rules, so that you can now set up almost any repayment schedule you want. You could require minimal payments in the early years, and heavier payments at the end. You could spread out the repayment period to 30 years if you wished.

By selling your property with a long-term note, you take the property out of your estate, and thus avoid estate taxes on it. Second, you minimize *income* tax consequences by having the payback schedule spread over a 30-year time period. The IRS requires the interest rate to be a reasonable reflection of the current market, but it does not have to match corporate rates. Inflation, which is likely to be substantially higher than the interest you receive, will gradually depreciate the value of the long-term note. This, of course, makes it much easier for your heirs to pay the note off. So in the end, you pay little or no tax on the property you sell to your heirs.

One of the problems with this arrangement, however, is that although your property is now outside your estate, the long-term note is still inside your estate. If you die before the note is paid off, the balance of the note remains in your estate. A way around this problem is to set up a "private annuity." When you sell your property to your heirs, for instance, have them pay you a monthly or yearly annuity for the rest of your life, based on actuarial tables. Then when you die, no further annuity payments are made—and your property belongs to your heirs, outside your estate.

Setting Up a Charitable Remainder Trust

A public charity—broadly defined to include colleges, churches, foundations, and other tax-exempt foundations—can offer tremendous tax breaks. Using a charitable remainder trust, it's possible to give away a substantial amount of money, receive a tax deduction, and still be able to use most of the money!

Here's how it works. You donate a piece of property or assets to your favorite college, church, foundation, or charity, using a charitable remainder trust. Under IRS rules, you're allowed to deduct 30% of the value of the contribution this year, with the balance carried forward into future years. You completely avoid any capital gains taxes.

In return, you will begin receiving a lifetime annuity from the charitable organization. The annual annuity payment must be at least 5% of the asset's value, and this annual annuity is considered taxable income. If the asset or property you donate is an inflation hedge (gold, silver, real estate, etc.), your annuity payments should increase with the cost of living.

One of the advantages of this technique is that you can design your own charitable program. Most tax-exempt organizations are very much aware of the tax advantages of charitable trusts, and are willing to arrange a program to fit your desires. You can make specific suggestions as to how you would like the charitable organization to use the money—for example, if you name your alma mater as the charitable trustee, you could request that it set up a chair of free-market economics, if that is a special interest for you.

There is one final alternative—set up your own public foundation to establish the charitable remainder trust. This would allow you to have full control of the money you contribute. As discussed in Chapter 9, the purpose of the foundation can be religious, educational, scientific, literary, or charitable. Many people might find this approach far more appealing than simply turning their property over to their children.

Pensions and Insurance

Pension and insurance proceeds can escape both income and estate taxes if properly planned.

Your pension plan—whether a corporate plan, Keogh plan, or Individual Retirement Account—can be passed on to your heirs without incurring estate taxes. The key is to have a *named beneficiary,* other than your estate, to receive the pension money.

Insurance proceeds are generally free from income taxes, but not necessarily from federal estate taxes. To avoid death taxes, you must avoid what the IRS calls "incidence of ownership." If there is any indication that you own or control the policy insuring yourself, the IRS will include the value of the policy in your estate.

There are several ways to make sure that insurance is not part of your estate. One way is for each spouse to purchase an insurance policy on the other. Premiums must be paid from separate, non-joint accounts, and the policies must be stored in separate, non-joint safety deposit boxes. The point is that the insured person cannot have any direct control over his insurance—he cannot pay premiums, have the right to change the beneficiaries, or have the right to borrow against the policy. These are known as "incidences of ownership."

Another approach is to establish an "irrevocable insurance trust." The trust must be irrevocable—you can't have any control over it, although you can choose your own trustee to act as a power of appointment. By setting up an irrevocable insurance trust—which requires annual federal reporting and a lawyer to set up—your insurance remains outside your estate.

Creative Gift-Giving

If you give a sizable gift to someone, even to your own child, the recipient does not have to declare it as income on his tax return. As the giver, you may not declare a deduction on your own return, unless the recipient is a tax-free entity (church, school, etc.). Moreover, if you give more than the federally exempt amount, you must pay a tax on the gift. Until 1981, you could give only $3,000 a year to any individual without incurring a gift tax liability.

But the new gift tax rules have greatly increased the exemption level. You can now give $10,000 to anyone without paying a gift tax. You cannot normally take a deduction for the gift, although corporations can deduct up to $25 per gift; and the recipient still would not have to claim the gift as income.

The $10,000 gift tax exclusion applies to each individual, so a husband and wife together can give up to $20,000 to each child each year if they wish to, without incurring a tax liability. Systematic gifts allow wealthy parents to transfer their estate to their heirs gradually, reducing the size of the estate so that estate levies will be lower at the time of death.

There is a way to surpass the $10,000 limitation. You can pay tuition costs and medical expenses in addition to the annual $10,000 without paying a gift tax! Payments must be direct, however; they cannot go through the beneficiary. Make sure, for example, that school tuition goes directly to the school, and that medical expenses are paid directly to the doctor or hospital. This additional exclusion is available to anyone; the recipient does not need to be your child, or even a relative, to qualify.

There are many alternatives to the kinds of gifts you can give. Many parents and grandparents give stocks and bonds to their descendants. In addition, the Uniform Gift to Minors Act makes it very easy to open a brokerage account, money market fund, or mutual fund on behalf of children or grandchildren. Your broker or mutual fund will provide you with the necessary forms.

You can maintain control over your investments while still passing them on to your heirs or donees free of gift, estate, or income taxes. Buy gold and silver coins—silver dollars, $20 gold pieces, etc.—and put them in a secure safety deposit box. Leave a notarized statement in the box along with the coins, certifying that you transfer these coins by gift to specific individuals. Make sure you sign and *date* the note. Also be sure that the market value of the coins does not exceed $10,000 per person per year. Finally, you must inform the recipient of the gift.

This technique is perfectly legitimate, especially if the recipients are not of legal age. Your safekeeping of the coins is completely warranted because of the need for security. When you die, these coins can be physically transferred to the rightful owners free of all taxes.

PLAN YOUR ESTATE NOW

The government estimates that 99.7% of all estates will be able to avoid federal estate taxes by 1987—a major victory for the taxpaying public. This high percentage may be optimistic, however. Double-digit inflation is still a growing, if not permanent, problem in our economy, and that fact will push many estates over the exemption level before long. Heirs may still be subject to *income* taxes when they sell inherited property. Moreover, the states still need to decide to what extent they will reduce their own death and gift rates. It is hoped that they will follow the federal government's incentive.

You need to reexamine your estate planning, in light of the new tax laws. Take maximum advantage of the new exemption level, which rises to $600,000 per person by 1987. If your estate surpasses the exemption level, look at the alternatives mentioned in this chapter, including having insurance owned by the beneficiary or by a trust, selling property to heirs using long-term notes, and transferring assets to heirs or to a public foundation, school, or charity gradually, while you still can. Even if you have no estate tax problem, you may wish to consider some of these techniques. A great deal of pleasure, and peace of mind, can come from a well-planned will that reflects your personal desires and altruistic spirit.

Problem Solver #10

Q. I have a large estate consisting of some properties and a few investments, together worth almost $1 million. Now that Reagan's tax law has passed, will I have to worry about federal estate taxes?

A. Not if you arrange your affairs properly. You can leave your entire estate to your surviving spouse and avoid federal estate taxes for the time being. But what happens when your spouse dies? The estate will pay sizable estate taxes then unless you do some planning now. Here are several possibilities. You could sell some of your property to your children, relatives, or friends, using a long-term note or a private annuity (make it a "joint" annuity if you want income to continue to your surviving spouse). Inflation will gradually make the note worth less and less. Set up a charitable remainder trust with your favorite charity, church, or educational institution. That way you can get a tax deduction as well as future income. You may even consider setting up your own private charitable foundation. Finally, giving annual gifts of $10,000 or less will avoid the gift tax.

12

—Tax-Free Barter

DURING THE Great Depression of the 1930s, very few people had ready cash. Businesses had to cut back on employees, throwing potential customers out of work. Goods and services were still available, but few had any money to pay for them. Prices fell sharply.

But a few enterprising souls realized that they could still produce and exchange goods and services, despite the lack of cash customers. Cooperatives were formed, allowing members to exchange their surpluses for items they needed. A few dozen eggs might buy a man's shirt; a house-painting job might purchase medical attention for a serious illness. Some co-ops became very complex, so that A might give a haircut to B, who would fix a broken fence for C, who would do a week's laundry for A. A system of credits and debits facilitated exchanges. When the depression ended, all were glad to see the return of a cash economy again, but the age-old principle of barter gained a new popularity that has not left us since.

Over the past few years, we have witnessed a dramatic resurgence of interest in barter exchanges, both formally through exchange clubs and informally among friends, neighbors, and business associates. The IRS assumes that escaping taxation is the primary reason for barter organizations, but representatives of these organizations tend to emphasize the economic advantages instead. They contend that barter is an excellent way to reduce excess inventory, to create new business when the company is short on cash, and to deal with shortages and government-imposed price controls. On a more personal level, many household budgets are stretched through the use of baby-sitting co-ops and other service exchanges, substituting time for cash.

While all these arguments in favor of barter are legitimate and useful, I frankly believe that the strongest force behind the recent expansion in the barter movement is the "tax-free" advantage. As can be expected, few organized exchanges are willing to discuss this sticky issue.

It would be a mistake to assume that all barter transactions are taxable, despite what some tax advisers, and the IRS, may have suggested. As in all tax situations, different circumstances produce different tax liabilities. On the other hand, it would be just as serious a mistake to assume that all barter transactions are tax-free. The truth lies somewhere in between. As Jesse Cornish once put it, "Tax advantages in barter resemble beauty, because they are in the eyes of the beholder." Barter is another example of the vast gray area in the tax code.

IS ALL INCOME TAXABLE?

In our effort to discover the black-and-white truth about barter transactions, we must first examine the definition of gross income, upon which taxes are based. The IRS tax guide *Your Federal Income Tax* states that "gross income includes all other income you receive—in the form of money, property or services—that is not, by law, expressly exempt from tax. . . . Income in any other form other than cash is reported at the fair market value of goods or services received."

"Fair market value"—ah, that's the rub. Now how does one define fair market value? Is it the retail price, the wholesale price, or is it any single price agreed on by the two parties involved in the exchange? The IRS tax guide states, "Fair market value is defined as the price at which the property would change hands between a willing buyer and a willing seller; neither being under any compulsion to buy or sell, and both having reasonable knowledge of the relevant facts."

This would indicate that all swapping agreements are taxable as ordinary income, right? Wrong! Again, fine distinctions are made, based on the circumstances and the products involved.

TAX-FREE PROPERTY SWAPS

There are numerous exceptions to this general definition of taxable income. Sections 1031 through 1040 of the Internal Revenue Code deal with "tax-free exchanges." These are defined as trades of investment or business property for "like kind" properties. You postpone the gain or loss on the exchange until you actually dispose of the new property for cash or for an "unlike kind" of property.

The IRS tax guide refers to several such trades: Real estate can be exchanged for real estate, an apartment house for a store building, or a machine for a truck. Vernon K. Jacobs, editor of *Tax Angles*, points out: "Investment property may be exchanged for business property—such as a rental building for a farm, or raw land for a factory building. Underdeveloped land may be exchanged for developed property. Various business properties such as trucks may be exchanged for other business equipment such as computers." Obviously "like-kind" exchanges are interpreted fairly broadly, and offer a wide opportunity for tax-free exchanges.

In every case, to qualify for the tax-free exchange, an actual exchange must be made, not a sale and purchase.

TAX-FREE BARTER OF COINS

There are also many "like-kind" exchanges allowed between investments. The IRS acknowledges the tax-free exchange of "like-kind" bullion coins, such as the Mexican 50 peso for the Austrian 100 Corona (Revenue Ruling 76-214). It even appears that gold bullion could be traded for silver bullion as a "like-kind" exchange. However, in Revenue Ruling 79-143, the IRS held that bullion-type coins could not be traded for numismatic coins as a like-kind exchange. Thus Krugerrands could not be exchanged for $20 double eagles on a tax-free basis, according to the IRS, which states that, "the bullion-type coins, unlike numismatic-type coins, represent an investment in gold on world markets rather than in the coins themselves." Numismatic coins, on the other hand, are valued according to their rarity, age, beauty, and history as well as for their gold content.

REAL ESTATE EXCHANGES

One of the most popular tax-free exchanges involves real estate. Since property values have increased spectacularly in the past couple of decades, the tax consequences of selling investment property can be substantial. Even though the rate on long-term capital gains has declined to a maximum level of 20%, many real estate investors are unwilling to pay hundreds of thousands of dollars to the government.

Suppose, for example, that you bought an office building a decade ago for $100,000, and that today the building could be sold for $300,000. If you sold the property, you would be able to deduct from the taxable gain both the sales commissions and the cost of any improvements you may have made. But, at the same time, if you have depreciated the building, you would have reduced the "cost basis" of the building, and thus increased your taxable gain. Let's say that the total taxable gain comes to $200,000, after costs and allowances. Since you owned the building for many years, it is a long-term capital gain, so only 40%, or $80,000, of the profit would be taxable. Assuming you're in the 50% tax bracket, that would result in a federal income tax of $40,000.

Most real estate investors are very reluctant to part with $40,000, even though they get to keep $160,000. They know that much of their profits are illusory because of inflation. So they seek to postpone the tax indefinitely through a property exchange.

Real estate investors are always looking for other pieces of property that might give them a better return, or greater diversification. Traditionally, they start searching for a like-kind exchange when the depreciation runs out, although some real estate speculators are always in search of new properties.

In the above example, the investor who wants to sell his office building will probably be looking for a larger piece of investment property, such as a large apartment complex, or even a bigger office building. In most like-kind property exchanges, the investor is looking for two essential things: (1) the new property must have a higher price; and (2) the new property must have a bigger mortgage. The negotiations can be extremely complex, involving buyers, sellers, banks, and several brokers. Needless to say, many real estate brokers dislike property exchanges because of the headaches, paperwork, and time involved. Other real estate brokers, as well as attorneys and title insurance companies, specialize in tax-free exchanges of real estate. Problems arise because the value of each property is never equal, and because the mortgages on each property are never equal. In most cases, cash makes up the difference.

Let's suppose that the office-building owner finds a $1 million apartment complex for sale. He persuades the apartment owner to make a tax-free exchange rather than a taxable sale. But the apartment owner really doesn't want the office building. No problem! The office-building owner finds a buyer for the building. When the exchange takes place, the office-building owner gets his apartment complex, the new buyer gets his office building, and the apartment owner gets *cash* from some newly created mortgages. You can see how complex the whole transaction can be. That's why whole books have been written on the subject.

PERSONAL PROPERTY EXEMPTIONS

Most personal property swaps are tax-exempt because in most cases personal property is *used* property, and has depreciated in value.

Most people are surprised to learn, for example, that proceeds from a garage sale are not taxable income. You would not have to declare any income gained from the garage sale because, in all likelihood, the earnings you receive from the sale will be vastly lower than the original cost of the items. This applies to the sale of used automobiles as well, except in the case of some antique autos that have increased in value. Any personal item you sell in the classifieds would not normally be taxable.

Consequently, if you swapped personal property for other personal property, the transactions should be tax-free. Some people have thought that when they sell a personal item for less than they paid for it, they should be able to take a loss on their tax return. But IRS won't allow a loss on personal property except in the case of a casualty loss.

Home exchanges are another area that may be exempt. Suppose you offer your home for two weeks, in exchange for someone else's home, possibly located in a vacation resort. Are you liable for tax on the fair market value income you could have earned if you had rented your home instead? Probably not; in this case, you are merely reducing the cost of your vacation while assuring that your own home will not remain empty while you are away.

BUSINESS BARTER

Many businesses will exchange similar products or services without incurring a tax liability. For example, when a publishing company trades its mailing list for another firm's mailing list, the trade is considered a "like-kind" transaction. Even though the company earns income from the mailing list it received, that income is balanced by the cost of the mailing list it gave to the other company. In essence, the expense is deducted from the phantom income, and the result is a zero *net* cost for both companies.

EXCHANGE OF SERVICES

What if a lawyer wants his home painted, and a housepainter needs legal advice? They get together, either through a formal exchange club or through coincidental friendship, and barter their services. Are they liable for tax, and if so, how much? According to a recent IRS ruling (Revenue Ruling 79-24), the lawyer is supposed to count as income the "fair market value" of the paint job, and the painter, the value of the legal advice.

Yet there are some questions left unanswered. What if the lawyer and painter were friends? How could the IRS prove that their services were not mutual *gifts*, which are exempt from tax? Moreover, who is to decide the "fair market value" of the services rendered?

Under our "voluntary" tax system, the lawyer and painter are expected to estimate how much the income should be. Let's say that the lawyer normally charges $50 an hour. Is that a fair market value? Not necessarily. He may charge more for certain clients, depending on the technical nature and difficulty of the case, or less for widows, friends, and moderate-income clients. Perhaps he offers discounts from time to time. On other occasions, he donates his time and services to charity. In other words, it is up to the lawyer and painter to decide for themselves what the value of the exchange is.

It simply isn't possible for the IRS to involve itself in such a confusing situation, particularly if it occurs as an isolated case. In the words of Vern Jacobs, "In our opinion, a good tax lawyer could have a field day with an attempt by the IRS to place a value on a pure exchange of services."

BARTER CLUBS

However, there would be a more serious problem if the swapping of services is done on a large, organized scale, as in the case of membership in an exchange club. Many barter organizations have developed a "check" or "credit" program, where monetary values are assigned to various barter transactions. Whenever these credits are used by a club member, the amount is recorded on the club's central computer bank, from which an administrative fee is charged by the organization. These credits are usually assigned at or near retail levels, which may or may not be a fair representation of value for value. Since, in most cases, these are neither like-kind exchanges nor related business expenses, they are considered taxable income at their fair market value.

Membership and service fees imposed by clubs are, of course, deductible, because they represent expenses related to finding barter partners, or customers. Additionally, many members feel that they can declare only a percentage of the retail "credit" value without any tax problem. For example, members might declare only between 25% and 75% of the "credit" value, depending on the circumstances and the aggressive approach of the participant.

A few informal barter clubs do not have a central computer, or a "credit" system. They simply charge a flat annual fee for the monthly newsletter, which provides a list of members, along with the items they want to exchange.

The IRS has sought the membership lists of some organized barter clubs, to check the "credit" records for possible underreporting of income by some members.

EXCHANGING SERVICES FOR PROPERTY

Finally, what about exchanging services for property? If a doctor trades his skills for a year's supply of eggs from the local grocer, must he report this non-cash transaction? According to the official IRS position, the answer is yes. As a practical matter, the IRS isn't likely to prosecute on small personal transactions, but if they become frequent and substantial, the barter trade is reportable.

"Fair market value" remains an uncertain area, open to interpretation. A company president may choose his own form of accounting, using the "wholesale" price to reduce income or the "retail" price to increase expenses. Check with your tax adviser to decide the best course of action. If there is a tax liability, try to reduce the value of the property to its *lowest reasonable value.*

WARNINGS ON IRS AND BARTER

As I have stated in this chapter, many barter transactions are completely tax-free, and others can legitimately be declared at low values. But because barter by its nature is hard to track, the IRS has recently attempted to crack down on "abusive" barter deals. The new *Audit Technique Handbook for Internal Revenue Agents* calls for special attention to be paid by agents to barter arrangements. They are to be alert to swapping techniques, especially those handled through "reciprocal trade agencies."

Agents are told to ask taxpayers if they have been engaged in any bartering, or have traded services for inventory or for "personal goods and services, such as vacations, houseboats, luxury cars, use of vacation home or condominium, or payment of personal or stockholder debts." If the answer is yes, be prepared to show and defend all your records concerning the transactions.

The case of Karl Hess and the IRS is an interesting tale. Hess was once a conservative speechwriter for Barry Goldwater, but has since become a libertarian involved in the "back to the land" movement. Philosophically opposed to all taxation, he refused to pay any taxes. His experience points out the trouble the IRS has had in collecting taxes from people who trade almost exclusively in barter. Hess writes:

> The tax collectors, hoisting their Jolly Roger high, placed a 100% lien upon my property and my earnings. I cannot, by their dictate, ever again earn a salary (they would take every penny of it) or own a thing. So be it. The resistance is my decision. The total assault is their decision. We must live with it. I do. And one way

I do it, is by barter. I am a welder, and a writer, and a metal sculptor. My welding is exchanged with my neighbors for many day-to-day needs of life in the Appalachian countryside where I live. My sculpture, most notably, is exchanged for the legal services with which I attempt to deal with the tax collectors as they expand their harassment of me to include my family and my friends. Some of the writing, however, is done for cash. Unfortunately, in an economy so dominated by the bookkeeping of credit and debit and speculation it is impossible to do some things (travel on public carriers is an example) without money. When I do receive cash, I spend it quickly or, if unable to, give it away. I have no place to store it except my pants pocket and I have a sneaking suspicion that the tax collectors have some sort of radar scanning that poor old pocket day and night, so obsessed do they seem with enforcing their 100% lien (an obsession notably absent in their gentle treatment of more prominent and powerful debtors).

Thus, from Hess' experience, we see that a person could live entirely from barter transactions, but that the system is both troublesome and costly at times. On a limited scale, however, it can prove to be valuable.

LOW-PROFILE BARTER: A SUMMARY

Barter is a difficult art to practice in a money economy, but it is growing in interest due to high rates of inflation and taxes. It is often an inefficient way to transact business, but in certain circumstances, particularly when cash is tight, it makes sense. Many forms of barter, including like-kind property exchanges and used personal property, are tax-free. Other exchanges may be taxable at their fair market value.

Problem Solver #11

Q. I have a profitable livestock business, but I would like to get out and do something else for a change. I was thinking of selling the farm and buying some garden apartments. I could sell the farm for a $100,000 profit, but

I hate to pay $20,000 in taxes, even if it is long-term capital gains. Any solutions?

A. How about a tax-free exchange, a farm for garden apartments? Investment property can be exchanged for business property under IRS rules. It could probably be arranged, although it might require third-party negotiations. The extra trouble would certainly be worth the tax savings.

13

— How to Defer Taxes Indefinitely

TOTALLY TAX-FREE living may seem unattainable to readers whose personal situations prevent them from taking advantage of the ideas outlined in this book. But tax *deferral* is readily available to nearly every American. And through a little creative planning, deferral can continue indefinitely, making your investments virtually tax-*free*.

Tax deferral is essential in today's financial environment. *It is the basic principle behind most tax shelters,* which offset current income with hefty deductions.

It is also necessary to *growing businesses,* which may show no profits at all, on paper at least, for the first five or six years, when heavy capital investment is essential to continued growth.

Real estate investors use heavy amounts of borrowed money, depreciation figures and credits, and like-kind exchanges to postpone their day of reckoning with the revenue man.

In sum, tax deferral is a way of life if you wish to survive in a world of high inflation and high taxation. This book has highlighted some investments and sources of income that are absolutely *tax-free,* but by far the majority of techniques are only *tax-deferred.* You don't have to pay taxes on your current return, but someday in the future you will have to declare the gain. Sometimes you may feel as though you're digging a hole that gets deeper and deeper, and you wonder if you'll ever escape. It's easy to make your financial life more complex as the years go by.

But through creative planning, calm analysis, and wise decisions, you can avoid taxes and still retain peace of mind. Some tax-deferral methods have been highlighted in previous chapters of this book. Pension programs, real-estate exchanges, temporary trusts, etc., have already been discussed. In this chapter, we will examine other ways to postpone taxes, perhaps indefinitely! After all, tax-*deferred* is as good as tax-*free* if taxes can be postponed forever!

THE VALUE OF APPRECIATED INVESTMENTS

When you purchase a non-income-producing asset, such as gold coins, growth stocks, or unimproved property, you have no tax liability until you sell the asset. Suppose, for instance, that you bought ten gold Krugerrands at $200 per coin several years ago. As long as you keep the coins, you do not owe any money to the government. They could be worth $2,000 per coin in a few years, as inflation worsens worldwide, but you would still owe no tax, even though the coins—or growth stocks, land, or collectibles—are worth many times what you paid for them. In essence, you have found a way to substantially *increase your net worth* without incurring any further debts to the government.

But what happens the day you decide to "take profits," whether to spend the money or to make another investment? The consequences aren't so bad. You're taxed at long-term capital gains rates, if you held the asset for more than one year. Thus, only 40% of the gain is taxable income, so even if you are in the 50% tax bracket, the maximum tax rate on the gain is 20%.

Advantages of Borrowed Money

Another alternative is to *borrow* against the appreciated asset, rather than to sell it. This method is growing in popularity, especially during an inflationary environment. If the cost of living is rising at 12% annually, and you can borrow money at 12%, you haven't lost anything by going to the bank.

Some appreciated investments are easier to borrow against than others. Gold coins and collectibles have limited possibilities, while income-producing real estate and stocks are commonly used as collateral. Margin accounts at brokerage houses are very easy to take advantage of when it comes to borrowing money. The Cash Management Account at Merrill Lynch, for instance, allows you to borrow money against your stocks at any time, simply by writing a check! You can borrow up to 50% of the value of your stocks. If you had $100,000 in stocks, you could borrow $50,000 at any time, no questions asked. Moreover, you could use the money for virtually any purpose, including the purchase of gold coins, collectibles, real estate, or an automobile. As long as you borrow against the value of your securities or assets, the money is not taxable. *Borrowed money is not taxable income!*

Owning appreciated assets will also increase your credit rating, allowing you to qualify more easily for *personal loans* without having to put up collateral. The bank's loan officer will look at your increased net worth as a major criterion for giving you an increased line of credit or a personal loan. Generally the appreciated asset will not be required as collateral.

The use of borrowed money is a fundamental principle in real estate investing. As property values have increased over the past decades, savvy real estate speculators have refinanced their present properties to purchase even more real estate. In some cases, they have taken part of the borrowed money in cash for living expenses—all without current tax liability. As Vernon K. Jacobs, editor of *Tax Angles*, states, "Money received as a loan is not regarded as income. Nor is the unrealized increase in the value of property. Put them together and it is possible for some people to borrow continually against the increased value of various properties and live off the loan proceeds. Of course, the value of the property must be increasing at a rate greater than the rate of interest being paid on the loans. But it is done fairly frequently."

It may seem impossible that a buyer could walk away from settlement with more cash than the seller, but many promoters of real estate courses, such as Al Lowry and Robert Allen, have taught how to put money in your pocket by using "creative financing" tools. Needless to say, there are significant risks to this approach. Real estate speculators have been caught in depressed market conditions from time to time, and many of them have gone from riches to rags, almost overnight.

THE ALL-AMERICAN TAX SHELTER

Your own home can offer some incredible financial benefits. Single-family houses have had a steady rise in value over the years, and are far more stable than any other kind of real estate investment. At the same time, the government permits you to sell your home and postpone any taxes on the gains from the sale if you buy a new home within two years. This tax deferral can become a permanent tax exemption when you reach age 55. At that point, or at any time thereafter, you can sell your home, and take up to $125,000 of the profits tax-free. You can then move to a smaller house or condominium, or rent—and use the $125,000 for investing. This tax-free exclusion is available only once, but the amount is likely to increase with inflation.

There are ways to use your home's equity before age 55, too. You can take out a second mortgage on the home at any time. In fact, many banks encourage these loans. Use the borrowed money for practically any purpose, including vacations, home improvements, investments, college education, etc. I strongly believe that the money should be used for investment or educational purpose only, however, not for a vacation or for personal expenditures. Use your money wisely for something that will pay dividends in the future.

ANNUITIES AND CASH-VALUE LIFE INSURANCE

Another major tax-deferral technique involves the use of life insurance products. Cash-value insurance has benefited from favorable legislation over the years. The cash values in a whole life policy accumulate tax-free. You can borrow against the cash value at low interest rates, and never pay it back if you don't want to—all tax-free. When you die, your named beneficiary can receive the face value of the policy without incurring income taxes. But remember that any outstanding loans will be deducted from the money your beneficiary receives.

The benefits of cash-value insurance simply don't outweigh the disadvantages, however. I firmly believe that *annual renewable term insurance* combined with a sound investment program is the best way to secure your financial future while providing protection for your dependents if you die. There are excellent term policies that can last your full lifetime and that are much cheaper than cash-value insurance over the long run.

The investment program that you may wish to use in connection with your insurance policy might include an *annuity program.*

These are essentially tax-deferred savings programs offered by insurance companies. They allow you to invest in a wide variety of investments that earn interest, dividends, and capital gains free of current taxes. You postpone all tax obligations until you make a withdrawal. And by using some simple techniques, you may be able to postpone taxes indefinitely. The IRS recently gave its sanction to a wide variety of annuities—including those that invest in the stock market—as long as the annuities do not invest in mutual funds that are available to the public.

These annuity programs are very flexible. You can invest in them for a few years, and then withdraw your money at any time. You are *not* required to "annuitize," i.e., enter into an agreement with the insurance company to pay you a lifetime monthly income. That option is available, but it is not mandatory, and frankly, I don't recommend it because of the inflationary environment in which we live. *Swiss franc annuities* are a lone exception, because the appreciation of the franc offers an opportunity for U.S. retirees to beat inflation. If you do choose to receive annuity payments, only the interest portion (as figured by IRS tables) is taxable, not the return of principal.

Here is a list of the major types of annuities on the market today:

• *Single-premium fixed annuities.* These are savings plans that pay you a specified interest return on a monthly basis. You make a single payment, and the interest paid on that amount is "fixed" every month or quarter, depending on the program. Usually a minimum guaranteed interest is offered. Recently these annuities have been paying 10–14% annually. Interest yields tend to follow national interest rates, so you should stay close to the inflation rate. Insurance companies impose withdrawal penalties of 4–6% during the first few years of the policy. If you wish to add to your annuity, you must initiate a new contract.

For a popular example of a single-premium annuity, write Q-PLAN, Anchor National Life Insurance Company (Camelback at 22nd St., Phoenix, AZ 85016). Anchor's annuity products are also sold by many brokerage firms.

• *Money market fund annuities.* Fidelity offers annuities that invest in money market securities, which have earned up to 14% in the recent past. Yields fluctuate daily, and the fund managers take about 1% annually for administrative fees. You can also invest in government or corporate bonds if you wish. For details, write: Fidelity Income Plus, P.O. Box 832, 82 Devonshire St., Boston, MA

02103; or call 800-225-6190, or, from within Massachusetts, 617-523-1919.

• *Stock market annuities.* Several insurance companies have combined with major mutual fund managers to form annuity products that invest in stocks and bonds. All interest, dividends, and short-term capital gains are completely free of current federal income taxation. However, the government imposes a 20% withholding tax on long-term capital gains achieved in the annuity unless it is part of a retirement plan. Because of this, annuity managers are developing ways to avoid long-term gains in the annuity funds. Best of all, you can decide how the money is invested. Here is a way to speculate and *aggressively trade* stocks and bonds on a tax-deferred basis, using annuities.

With these "investor-directed variable annuities," you have a choice of several funds—funds that specialize in aggressive growth stocks, corporate or government bonds, income-producing stocks, or safe money market securities. You can switch from one fund to another at any time without paying taxes or penalties. There are, of course, administrative fees and extra expenses, however—usually amounting to 1–2% of your investment each year. But it's not a high price to pay for tax-free investing!

You can find out more about these "variable annuities" by contacting a major brokerage house (Merrill Lynch, Bache, Dean Witter, etc.), or by contacting the following companies directly: Spectrum Annuity, Massachusetts Financial Services of Boston, 200 Berkeley St., Boston, MA 02116; Keystone 100 Annuity (Keystone Massachusetts Inc., 99 High St., Boston, MA 02110); Value Guard (Guardian Life Insurance Co. of America, 201 Park Ave. S., New York, NY 10003).

Unlike single-premium annuities, most of the variable annuities permit you to add to the account at any time without having to establish a new contract.

A newsletter that monitors and makes specific recommendations on stock market annuities is available from Dick Fabian, *Telephone Switch Newsletter* (P.O. Box 2538, Huntington Beach, CA 92647; $97 a year). He uses a very simple system of technical trading that has resulted in substantial, consistent profits over the years. Mr. Fabian will send you a special report on "No-Load Investor-Directed Variable Annuities" for $5, or, if you subscribe, he will send it to you free. Most "family funds" allow telephone switching features, but switching between funds within an annuity can only be executed by mail.

New Taxes on Withdrawals

You can let your money accumulate for a long period of time before you have to make withdrawals. Not until age 80 do you have to start taking money out, or begin an annuity-for-life plan.

It used to be that you could withdraw your original principal without any tax consequences, but the new 1982 tax law treats initial withdrawals as taxable-interest income.

The new law also discourages borrowing against annuities. Loans using annuities as collateral will be treated as taxable income.

In addition, a new 5% penalty is imposed within the first 10 years of an annuity contract for withdrawals made prior to age 59½.

All of these measures were pushed by the IRS, and incorporated into the 1982 tax reform act because annuities had become a popular tax shelter.

One thing you can do is roll over your U.S. annuity into a Swiss annuity, if you have reached retirement age. You could set up a guaranteed monthly income for life in Swiss francs, which have appreciated against the dollar over the years. If you had purchased a Swiss annuity that paid $1,000 a month in 1970, today you would be receiving over $2,500 a month! Using IRS tables, you would have to declare a certain portion of the monthly income as interest and be taxed accordingly.

A London insurance broker, Robert Edgar, helps his clients to borrow against Swiss franc endowments. An endowment policy is like a certificate of deposit, except that it's issued by an insurance company; you make a deposit with the insurance company and it pays you a lump sum, principal plus interest, at the end of a specified time period, usually 2–10 years. Normally, an endowment policy also carries insurance for one to two times the face value of the policy, but this is an option. Interest is tax-deferred until paid. Of course, if you want to defer taxes for a longer period of time, you can exchange your old endowment or annuity contract for another one tax-free (IRS Section 1035).

Edgar recommends that his clients invest in a Swiss franc endowment, and then he has them borrow 95% of the endowment policy for further investment purposes such as gemstones, gold, etc., depending on market conditions.

Minimum investment is typically around $10,000. For details on Swiss annuities and endowments, write the following services:

Robert Edgar, Director
Edgar Ward Ltd
15 Minories
London EC3N 1NJ, England

Assurex S. A.
P.O. Box 290
8033 Zurich, Switzerland

International Insurance Specialists
P.O. Box 949
1211 Geneva 3, Switzerland

SERIES E BONDS

Series E bonds, or government savings bonds, have a unique characteristic, in that you can postpone the tax on the accumulated interest until you redeem the bond. Currently Series E bonds are paying a substantial return compared to previous years, but they still don't compare to yields available on other tax-deferral investments such as annuities, and are therefore not recommended.

POSTPONING TAXES: PROS AND CONS

Pension plans, annuities, equity loans, and other investments can be used to postpone taxes for a long period of time. But should you? There are several advantages. First, you keep a larger amount of funds for investing and living. You can earn interest, dividends, or capital gains on these deferred funds. The compounding effect can be a tremendous gain for you over many years.

Second, inflation destroys the value of the dollar over time, which means that when you do finally pay taxes, you pay in highly inflated dollars. Today's tax dollar is worth a great deal more than a dollar will be worth a decade from now. Consequently, it pays to pay later.

Finally, you can arrange for many of these tax-deferred investments to be passed on to your heirs free of federal income or estate taxes. This is true of both pension plans and annuities. Make sure your named beneficiary is someone other than your "estate." At that point you will have turned your tax deferral into a tax exemption.

Problem Solver #12

Q. In these times of uncertainty, I have all my investment funds earning high interest in a money market fund. Last year I earned $8,000. I don't need the income for current living expenses, but I hate giving so much of it to the government. How can I earn high *tax-free* interest without losing to inflation?

A. Tax-deferred annuities may be one solution. If you don't need the interest income, but you want to keep up with inflation, annuities are a good alternative. The interest return tends to keep up with national interest rates. If inflation worsens, interest rates will tend to rise. If interest rates are rising sharply, money market annuities are best because the yield changes daily.

Another alternative may be a Swiss franc endowment through a Swiss insurance company. This is a very private way to earn tax-deferred income in a hard currency, one that will probably do much better at keeping ahead of inflation than a U.S. tax-deferred annuity.

14

—The Magic of Tax Shelters: How to Convert Ordinary Income into Long-Term Capital Gains

ALTHOUGH THIS book specializes in the area of tax exemptions, it is valuable to discuss tax shelters as a way to defer taxes into the future and eventually convert ordinary income into tax-favored long-term capital gains. Moreover, tax shelters are absolutely essential if you are still working and receiving "earned" income. Without them, it won't be long before you will be paying half your money to the government.

Most tax shelters are in the form of *limited partnerships,* in which numerous investors pool their funds with a general partner to invest in a particular project. You can form a tax shelter on your own, but many investors don't have the necessary capital or borrowing power to fund an entire project.

Limited partnerships are sold by tax-shelter brokers. Public issues are registered with the Securities and Exchange Commission and are generally sold by major brokerage houses. Private placements, typically involving 35 or fewer investors, are not registered with the SEC, and are generally sold by independent tax-shelter promoters. Private placements usually offer high write-offs, greater risks, and more profit potential than public offerings.

THREE BENEFITS TO TAX SHELTERS

Tax shelters offer several financial benefits to the limited partners.

High Tax Deductions

First, you obtain a high deduction on your income tax return for the amount of money invested. It is not unusual to get a $20,000 deduction when you invest $10,000 in a tax shelter. A real estate partnership, for example, can give you this kind of deduction. In tax-shelter terminology, this is called a 2-to-1 write-off. Most conservative shelters offer 100% write-off or less; aggressive shelters can offer as high as 4-to-1 write-offs. I do not recommend tax shelters offering better than 2-to-1 because these projects are usually very risky and have little or no economic justification. If the shelter is audited, the IRS will probably disallow some or all of the deductions.

Economic Profits in the Future

Second, a tax shelter offers a future economic profit which can be substantial. Many partnerships have shown sizable profits of 400–500% over several years. A real estate project may have profited from a real estate boom; an oil and gas exploration project may have made substantial discoveries; a movie might become an overnight success; a cattle-breeding operation may have sold its herd at top prices.

But the risk of failure is also present. A gold-mining project may not pay out. A promising research and development deal may turn sour. A racehorse may prove to be a loser. A promoter may turn out to be a fraud. You take your chances. But overall, if you choose carefully and diversify into a variety of tax shelters, you are likely to make profits over the long run.

Ordinary Income Transformed into Capital Gains

Third, a tax shelter can turn ordinary income into long-term capital gains. Many tax shelters simply defer your tax liabilities. You receive tax deductions in the early years, and taxable income in the later years. Fortunately, some tax shelters not only give you early write-offs, but they also pay you income in the form of substantial capital gains that are taxed at very low rates, 20% or less. Let's look at some examples.

REAL ESTATE

Income-producing property offers you the chance to get sizable tax deductions in the early years for depreciation, interest, and real estate taxes, and long-term capital gains when you finally sell the property several years later. Many limited partnerships borrow money to buy an apartment complex, upgrade it, and sell it for a profit in four or five years. The general partner often takes a sizable fee and part of the profits in return for managing the property. Sometimes the fees and commissions are so large that only a full-scale real estate boom will result in profits for the limited partners. Watch out for high fees and commissions in a real-estate prospectus or offering memorandum.

CATTLE BREEDING

A cattle-breeding operation offers the chance for long-term capital gains when the larger herd is finally sold several years later. This is not a cattle-*feeding* operation, which is quite different and is only a one-year tax deferral. Cattle feeding means beefing up young cattle for sale the following year. Cattle breeding, on the other hand, is a long-term proposition. It consists mainly of cows and heifers, and a small number of bulls to service them. Depreciation, investment tax credits, and deductions for expenses and interest on commercial loans are taken, and several years later the full-grown cattle are sold for long-term capital gains, which are 60% tax-free. There is a risk involved, in that the profits on selling the cattle might not be sufficient to pay the expenses. Cattle-breeding operations are usually leveraged, meaning that the partners must take on a personal debt.

GOLD MINING

Gold-mining shelters have an interesting twist. If a gold-mining venture proves successful, a limited partner can receive a distribution in the form of *gold bullion* without having to pay any tax on the value of the gold! This is allowed because the gold bars are considered a distribution of "inventory" (IRS Tax Code Section 731). If you sell the gold, you will be taxed at ordinary income rates *unless* you have held the gold for at least five years. After five years, you can sell the gold for long-term capital gains.

While the tax benefits can be tremendous, the chief drawback to this shelter has been in finding a successful gold-mining venture. Very few have proved successful. Ranchers Exploration and Development Corp. of Albuquerque, N.M., had a successful public program, but it has no plans for marketing other gold-mining partnerships at the present time. A few private placements have paid out in gold, but until the price of gold recovers, it is unlikely that very many will be available. Investors should also beware of questionable gold-mining schemes that promise high write-offs and pie-in-the-sky profits.

TAX SHELTERS THAT GO PUBLIC

A final major category of favorable tax shelters involves limited partnerships that eventually convert to public shares. One of the drawbacks to most tax shelters is that the investor's money is tied up for years, and there is virtually no way to get out of a tax shelter unless the general partner is willing to buy your share. A technique growing in popularity has been to offer the tax shelter publicly, issuing shares in exchange for partnership interests.

For example, Magic Circle, a public limited partnership in oil and gas development, has offered in the past to convert partnership units into shares of Magic Circle Energy Securities Corp. Thus, tax-shelter investors could hold the stock for a year, and then sell for long-term capital gains.

A number of tax shelters, including oil and gas, research and development, etc., have the option of converting units into publicly traded shares, offering investors the chance to exit from the tax shelter and eventually sell for long-term capital gains.

VIRTUE AND VICE OF TAX SHELTERS

Too many tax shelters solve a tax problem only temporarily, and, in fact, make matters worse in the long run. They place you in a risky, illiquid, and indebted position. In some cases, they create "phantom income," money that you never see, but that is still listed as taxable income on your return.

The solution is to search for reputable, low-risk tax shelters that provide not only current tax deductions, but the opportunity to exit with high profits and low taxes.

RECOMMENDED READING

Brennan Reports, P.O. Box 822, Valley Forge, PA 19482; $100 for 12 issues. The best monthly newsletter on specific tax shelters, written by William Brennan.

Tax Angles, 1300 N. 17th St., Arlington, VA 22209; $60 for 12 issues. An excellent newsletter on tax-saving ideas; Vernon K. Jacobs, editor.

Problem Solver #13

Q. I'm just starting to earn good money. My problem is finding ways to shelter my income before I'm taxed to death. Last year I earned $25,000, and paid $5,000 in taxes. Unfortunately, I don't make enough to invest in a limited partnership. Most brokers expect you to be well-to-do, and able to make an investment of $10,000 or more. How about a tax shelter for someone with just $5,000 in savings?

A. There is a solution to your tax problem. True, you may not have the funds to get into a cattle-breeding operation, an oil and gas deal, or some other limited partnership. But how about buying a small piece of income-producing property, purchased on your own with a small down payment? There are numerous opportunities available if you shop around carefully. Let's suppose you find a small house in need of repair in a nice neighborhood. The owner wants out, and is willing to sell it for $50,000, if you are willing to put 10% down. You pay him $5,000, and he takes back a long-term note at 12% interest. Your monthly mortgage payment comes to $470 a month, which includes insurance. You make some cosmetic improvements and rent the house.

This small investor's tax shelter will sharply reduce your tax liability this year. Even if you can only rent the house for an amount equal to your monthly mortgage payment, the depreciation on the house can amount to almost $5,-000. That extra $5,000 tax deduction is enough to bring your tax bracket down to a much lower level.

After renting and making home improvements for a few years, you can sell the house and take a long-term capital gain, perhaps buying another house or two with the profits. Real estate fortunes have been made this way.

15

—How to Minimize Your Taxes: Advice for Investors, Businessmen, Executives, and Retirees

EACH OF us has different wants, needs, assets, income levels, and priorities. To some people, living near family and friends in a traditional hometown is a strong desire; to others, working at a certain occupation provides pleasure beyond the monthly paycheck. Still others feel that constant change is essential to an adventurous life. But while each individual is unique in some ways, all of us have one thing in common: We all want to minimize our costs. Since taxes take one-third of the average American's income, reducing tax expenditures becomes a paramount goal.

Whether you are an executive, a professional, a salaried employee, a wage-earner, an expatriate, or self-employed, you can reduce your tax bill. In this chapter, I will summarize ways in which you can profit from the ideas set forth in this book.

THE PRIVATE INVESTOR

Everyone belongs in the category of "investor." Whether you have an elaborate investment program or just a passbook savings account, you are an investor. How can you keep more of your profits?

Emphasize long-term capital gains. This is an essential principle of investing, yet it is surprising how few investors remember to do it. Most of their money may be tied up in money market funds, or in dividend-paying stocks and bonds. Yet, in an inflationary environment, the real money is being made in *capital investments* that pay little or nothing in dividends. Small, budding companies in computers, high technology, and manufacturing—companies that didn't pay a dime in dividends, but whose stocks quadrupled in value—have outperformed the market over the past decade.

What kinds of investments have profited from the government-induced inflation of the past two decades? Precious metals, rare coins, hard currencies, and collectibles have increased in value, although they never paid any dividends. Contrast this return on capital investments with the income-producing blue-chip stocks and bonds, which declined sharply during this inflationary binge.

Not only do capital investments stay ahead of inflation over the long term, but their profits are taxed at very low rates—a maximum of 20% under the new law. This can represent a significant tax savings.

Take a close look at your *investment portfolio.* Are you receiving *income* you don't need for current living expenses? In my experience as an investment adviser, I have seen countless clients with too much money in dividend-paying stocks, bonds, and money market funds. They may be reluctant to sell for a variety of reasons. Perhaps they want safety and a steady return, so they invest in a money market fund. Blue-chip companies may seem more stable than smaller companies. They may not wish to sell their stocks because of the tax consequences. All of these reasons have merit. But you should realize that in addition to their favorable tax rates, investments which increase your net worth rather than your gross income will also *reduce* your chances for a tax audit, since the IRS computer tends to kick out returns of higher-income taxpayers for audit. I suggest that you review your portfolio and at least reduce your holdings of income-producing investments.

If you need income to live on, municipal bonds, which are paying unprecedented high yields, are a possible alternative to taxable stocks, bonds, and money market funds. Some of the mutual funds even offer tax-free money market funds that invest in munies. These come with a check-writing privilege. The yield is lower, but the *after-tax* return may be higher for wealthy investors.

Income-splitting techniques, through gifts and interest-free loans to your family members, may be a good way to save thousands of dollars in income taxes.

Annuities are an excellent way to postpone taxes indefinitely. I strongly recommend them as a flexible way to play your tax-lowering strategy. The variable annuities permit you to speculate aggressively in some top mutual funds without paying current taxes.

Tax shelters, of course, cannot be ignored. They are a very useful tool for postponing and eliminating tax liabilities. Some, such as real estate, can turn ordinary income into favorable long-term capital gains. You should invest in some tax shelters in oil and gas, research and development, or real estate, if you have a high level of interest or dividends.

THE BUSINESSMAN OR COMPANY PRESIDENT

For the entrepreneur who has started his own company, or for the man who has worked his way up to becoming company president, there are many options available to help reduce tax obligations.

The foremost way to reduce taxes is through owning your own business. The president of a small company, who owns all or most of the stock in his corporation, can eventually sell the company for long-term capital gains. In essence, this becomes an effective way to turn ordinary income into long-term capital gains. Any businessman learns early in the game that it pays to keep a low salary, and to reinvest as much as possible into the company, both to promote growth and to lower taxes. Then, when he sells the company some day, the maximum tax on his gain is only 20%. Meanwhile, while he still owns the company, he can take advantage of many tax-exempt benefits. The fringe benefits described in Chapter 4 can be written so that they favor the owner and key executives, within the bounds set by IRS regulations. For example, insurance and pension benefits can be tied to the salary level of the employees, or can require a minimum length of service before an employee can qualify. Obviously, key executives earn considerably more than other employees, and therefore will obtain greater fringe benefits.

Many companies, especially smaller firms, have a wide variety of choices available to them when it comes to deciding where to locate their plant or main office. They can take advantage of the *state tax havens* and sometimes can even locate *offshore*. Industry is moving heavily into Texas, for example, because it has no personal or corporate income tax.

Small one-man companies that have great growth potential can also take advantage of stock recapitalization as an estate-planning tool. The company president holds on to low-priced preferred shares, while giving the common stock to his children. If the company grows into a multimillion-dollar operation, he will have successfully transferred the company's increased worth to his heirs, free of estate taxes.

I also recommend that presidents or principal owners of companies consider establishing their own tax-exempt organizations for charitable, scientific, or other public purposes. As I have shown, such a public foundation has tremendous tax advantages, and you can even have some of your employees work for the foundation, thus avoiding employment taxes. The foundation's goal can be very broad, enhancing the goodwill of the company.

SALARIED WORKERS AND WAGE-EARNERS

Employees also have many options available for reducing their tax burdens. One of the most overlooked sources of reduced-tax income is through working for a tax-exempt organization that does not participate in social security. A list of these organizations can be obtained from the IRS—it's public record. Job seekers would be wise to apply to several of these public organizations to find the best employment opportunity, since reducing taxes is not the only consideration by any means. Be sure to ask if the company participates in social security—some do, and some don't. These tax-exempt organizations often have many fringe benefits similar to those provided by private companies.

Working for the federal government can be a way of getting out of social security, and into an attractive pension program. Just make sure you have a job that really serves the public—so many federal jobs contribute to nothing but the growing tax burden.

One of the most interesting alternatives, especially for executives, is to work offshore for a foreign company. You can earn up to $75,000 free of U.S. taxes, while getting an additional deduction for housing costs. In most cases, you can escape U.S. social security taxes and state income taxes, although you may be liable for foreign social security and local taxes. Under the new tax law, I'm sure many new job opportunities will be opening up outside the United States. Many companies offer incredible fringe-benefit packages, including five or six weeks of paid vacation in the States!

During the middle years, when most people are experiencing their period of highest earnings, it pays to develop a solid long-term savings program. This plan should be twofold. First, you should have an investment portfolio *outside* your pension plan consisting chiefly of *capital assets* or *inflation hedges,* such as gold, silver, collectibles, real estate, foreign currencies, growth stocks, aggressive growth mutual funds, etc. These investments should provide good long-term gains at low tax rates. Second, you should have one or more IRS-approved pension plans, consisting of a corporate, Keogh, or individual retirement account. People who have a corporate or Keogh plan can also have an IRA. These investments should emphasize *high yields and short-term capital gains,* because all profits are taxed as ordinary income when they are withdrawn from a pension plan. I recommend money market funds, bonds, utilities, and *short-term* trading of stocks, mutual funds, gold shares, etc., holding them for less than one year. By dividing your long-term savings program this way, you will minimize your return while minimizing your taxes.

RETIREES

Most retirees are overly concerned with the desire for steady monthly income to supplement social security payments. They often opt for private pension plans, annuities, and an investment portfolio consisting of stocks, bonds, and money market funds. Because of this emphasis on income, the tax burden for retirees is surprisingly high—much higher than they were told it would be when they were working full-time.

My recommendation to retirees is: Don't rely too heavily on income sources to preserve your capital. Look toward capital gains. The retiree who bought a bag of silver coins in 1970 for $1,500 can now sell those coins for $8,000. When you need income for living expenses, simply sell a coin, gemstone, or stock that you have held for more than a year. You will have money in your pocket, and your tax liability will be 60% lower.

Municipal bonds should not be relied upon too heavily. They may offer good returns when interest rates are high, but they must not be purchased and then forgotten. If inflation resurfaces—almost a sure bet—these bonds will drop sharply in value. You must diversify!

One of the best investments that offers both income and capital appreciation is *South African gold shares.* Despite their political risks, they have proved to be an excellent inflation hedge for retirees. People who bought South African gold shares in the early 1970s have seen their *dividends* exceed the prices they paid for the shares! Of course, like any other speculation, gold shares go down in price as well as up—so you must be willing to become an "informed speculator."

What about moving to a foreign retirement haven, like Mexico, the Caribbean, Canada, or Europe? Many countries don't tax foreign residents on their U.S.-based income, but that doesn't eliminate the U.S. tax liability. The $75,000 tax exclusion applies only to *earned* income abroad, not to unearned income from annuities, investments, pensions, etc., which are often the main source of income for retirees. Still, many retirees wisely make money in part-time or even full-time jobs, so an overseas adventure may be a great way to retire.

What about state tax havens? Millions of retirement-aged individuals consider moving to another state, particularly to a warmer climate, when they finally retire from work. In the South, both Florida and Texas offer tempting tax advantages and balmy weather. Nevada offers exciting nightly entertainment in Las Vegas, Reno, and Lake Tahoe, in addition to the lure of no income taxes or estate taxes. Other havens include New Hampshire, and Washington State along the Oregon border.

Another principal concern of retirees is estate planning. The techniques outlined in Chapter 11 are extremely important in the case of large estates—and with inflation, most estates will become larger in the near future. Take advantage of installment sales, gift-giving, charitable trusts, beneficiary-owned insurance, and other estate-planning tools.

TAX FREEDOM IN AN UNFREE WORLD

In conclusion, then, you must always be on the lookout for ways to reduce your taxes. Once you pay them, the money is gone forever, and you certainly don't get it all back in government "services." It is both legal and ethical to eliminate or postpone your tax obligations as long as possible—through the *exemptions* that Congress has specifically written into the tax code.

If there is one lesson that you should have learned from reading this book, it is that taxation is not equal by any means. Whether we speak of individual investors, company organizations, states of the union, or countries of the world, there is a great disparity in the taxes required. It is up to *you* to take advantage of these disparities.

Excessive taxation deprives all of us of a basic freedom, the freedom to choose how we will spend the money we earn. Fortunately, you can reduce your tax burden so that, in the words of Harry Browne, you *can* find "freedom in an unfree world."

Index